# THE ONLY SOLUTION AGAINST THE GREAT RESET IS RIGHT IN OUR BIBLE

CHUCK DONNEL

*To all the brave, freedom-loving folks worldwide
who are standing up against tyranny in our existential
great struggle against the great reset*

# CONTENTS

# ACKNOWLEDGMENTS

To the One who Loved me and gave Himself for me. His constant encouragement and enlightenment in Scripture and current events has been everything, and I can honestly say that Jesus Christ of Nazareth deserves all credit. I have fallen in love with this unfathomable Savior who is always with me and reminds me to cast every care upon Him. His blood cleanses me from all unrighteousness, and saving me to the uttermost, and presents me blameless in His presence. My love and fear abound for the Father, Son and the Holy Ghost with Their powerful aid. Believing as a little child is difficult for such a self-sufficient male as myself, but with the crucifying power of Christ I can even overcome my flesh.

# INTRODUCTION

Civil war resistance to the great reset seems to be the sad perspective of many. Most are oblivious to God's solutions, and the ignorance of end-times Bible teachers has only furthered the enemy's plans. We need to rethink listening to these proclaimed experts who have cut out Israel's promises made to them by God's written Word. Most modern Bible teachers consider the Scriptures so complex that they need theology to explain them, yet their professed ignorance hasn't led them to become like little children, yoked together with the Author of the Scriptures to reveal their simple truths. Believing man is in charge of interpreting Scriptures is an open admission that they don't want Scriptures to rule over them but they want to rule over Scripture; that isn't going to end well.

It's been said, "perspective is everything." I would add: "Having God's perspective is everything." When I was miraculously saved in 1970, a great hunger for the New Testament soon followed. My journey through the Scriptures with the Author has been an absolute necessity in writing this book. Years later, I was told by God to read ten pages a day. On my eighth time through the entire Bible, I was given a clear, unassailable view of salvation and a powerful walk with Christ, not just from my experience but from the Bible itself, and a fairly clear view of God's working in biblical government with how that matches so much of early American government and how deviations from biblical solutions have failed. On about number 20 for the Old Testament and 40 for the New Testament, reading cover to cover, I was given a fairly clear view of what's to come; then, subsequently, a period of God's miraculously leading me through the Scriptures, seeing how everything fits together without contradictions.

A perfect understanding of all prophecy is extremely difficult if not impossible because of God's intent. One thing we must keep in mind is man's prideful intent to self-fulfill God's prophecies. That's why many prophecies make little sense until they are fulfilled, such as Jeremiah 31:15, which could have been self-fulfilling if it had been clearer, but instead it made no sense until Herod murdered all the little children in Bethlehem in an attempt to murder Jesus. If we keep reading, the next couple of verses are very clear that those kids will rise from the dead and come from the land of their enemies (Bethlehem is now under enemy control) to their own border. So as you can plainly see, the second part of this prophecy cannot be self-fulfilled by man, so God can talk plainly about it. So is it with most of the prophecies about Israel's physical and spiritual restoration—they are so supernatural that they are humanly impossible to replicate. Naturally it takes faith from the Author to believe these prophecies and the promises connected to them. Remember, without faith it is impossible to please Him (Hebrews 11:6). Israel's failures to actually trust God were the bases for God's punishments and oftentimes complete rejection of that generation, so when Hebrews 4:1 tells us to "fear lest a promise being left us from God that we haven't entered into," God is extremely serious!

This book has several distinct purposes, but overwhelmingly it is an attempt to get believers to see where we are in history according to the Bible prophecies and get them to start calling out to God for His promised vengeance on His enemies in order to restore Israel, America, and most of the world back to a living, holy relationship with Christ and powered by Christ, as promised by the parable of the fig tree, over eight hundred verses in the Old Testament, and over a hundred in the New Testament.

Enjoy reading. You'll be amazed how Scripture foretells the bioweapon jab, the Islamic hatred for America and Israel foretold and miraculously ended, the need for a great deliverance from the evil great reset, and many other events to come that have been ignored for decades by "churchianity." Prior to D. L. Moody, revivals in America focused on being saved, to follow Christ to make a better world by building the kingdom, such as establishing freedom for all including slaves, but the minds of the revivalists changed with Moody to see their role as saving souls from a sinking ship that was getting worse and worse. Teaching individual salvation without changing the nations is a clear violation of the Great Commission in Matthew 28, making the principle of praying "Thy will be done on earth as it is in heaven" completely void of meaning. Some voices countered such fatalistic preaching, such as General Booth, the founder of the Salvation Army, who feared a time of politics without God. The teachers union in 1900 bemoaned the church casting aside its responsibility of teaching our children and shifting that responsibility to government. This shift away from biblical preaching created a vacuum for government to become the savior of mankind, but a shift is happening today. Even our most successful conservative President Trump, in a Christmas message at a church in 2021, declared we need a savior, "and that Savior isn't me," as he put his hand on his chest, "but it's Him," as he pointed toward heaven. Jack Hibbs, a conservative preacher, has been quoting Charles Finney's famous sermon that squarely puts the blame on the ones who occupy the nation's pulpit for the departure from biblical living, both for congregations and our nation.

To the faithful believers who are grieved with the evil of our day: a simple fervent prayer for more of Christ and less of yourself will open a treasure chest of life. Something very helpful for those who feel Christ inside them is to ask Him to pray through you. The Scriptures mentioned in this book will prove to be a great eye-opener and comfort directly from God.

# CHAPTER 1

# COVID-19 Is Just the Smoke Screen

Our modern world is run by very powerful people in high places who would love to bring the entire world under their control. They are nefarious actors who will stop at nothing to bring about their dream, which is our nightmare, of one world government. Just like the magician diverts our attention with one hand to do his trick with his other, so COVID and the "vaccine" is a diversion for a worldwide collapse of economies and their dream of complete digital control of every person. This may seem strangely familiar to the mark of the beast in the Book of Revelation in the Bible, yet there are several missing components.

Ultimately, it's best to pinpoint, as best we can, where we are prophetically, which we will do in simple detail later in this book. This is the realization and openness to such realization, that satanic forces are trying to set up a one world government as they have many times since the Tower of Babel, not the famous antichrist that calls fire down from heaven as he speaks great blasphemies against God. The danger we're in right now is extremely scary, especially considering the power these forces have now, and if they obtain the USA military they would not leave a free country on the planet. The progress of freedom for the individual to live free of oppression is dwindling even as I speak: travel, private property rights, parents rights, abundance of food, and a host of everyday things we take for granted; even our own lives will be gone.

A growing distrust of government, churches, education, politics, science, media, and medical establishments is increasingly widespread. The growing skepticism in man's solutions has fueled a growing trust in the Bible's eternal truths along with the Author Himself to counter these evil, power-hungry maniacs.

The concept of people wanting such power, and brainwashing, bribing, blackmailing, or threatening other people to help them get this control, is foreign to our thinking. It's not something we want ourselves so we can't imagine others wanting it. Hitler was a master at manipulating media, and thus people, to do what he wanted. Free thinkers were simply ignored or eliminated. Actually, accusing your enemies of what you're really doing was invented by Hitler's control machine. Knowing what your enemies are doing and fighting against them with our judicial system, let's say, is admirable and expected of good people, but we need more than we have as humans. This book was not written to discourage any effort but rather to turn the tables on the enemy so he cannot win, and so God wins instead. Most would be happy to just return to 2019. Yep, happy times and much peace. But when we get close to God, we realize how far we were from Him and how much of a foothold the enemy had in our own lives and the nation. If we're going to win with God, we're obligated to work with God and His righteousness.

The thought that we can actually win against such powerful evil is taking an interesting turn in the people on the front lines. They seem to be running on some supernatural strength that keeps them going, and they are calling out for prayer for themselves and others injured in the battles. They seem to spend more time than ever before in their Bibles. They are often quoting right out of their Bible. The enormous sphere of power of the enemy has surprised each of them, but it has only made them stronger with more resolve. These times were predicted in Scripture, as we will see in more detail later, even down to the side effects of the jab.

As mentioned in the introduction, the style of preaching changed, and thus the effects of the preaching changed, eroding our faith in Christ and His plans for our world. Jesus declares all power has been given unto Him: "therefore go into all the world and make disciples of all nations, teaching them to observe all things I have commanded you." This isn't a sinking-ship attitude, but a "no king but King Jesus," as in the Revolutionary War; or, "as He died to make men holy, let us die to make men free," as at the Civil War. Driving evil off the earth isn't some hippie on drugs getting along with evil but rather the Christ who could boldly say, "Neither do I condemn you. Go and sin no more."

Our life in Christ is one that makes us more than conquerors, not caving in to every evil just to get along. Most of our pulpits have hired liars who refuse to call out sin within and without the church walls, but instead assure the itching ears that all is well between them and God. Judgment must begin at the household of God for real changes to take place in our country and the world. All power is not just words in a song that leaves the singer powerless against evil in their own lives and the world, but rather exactly as Christ said and commanded. Paul negates all governments that are not a terror to evil in Romans 13. Our own Declaration of Independence separates from England because of its tyranny against good, thus giving our revolution forebears just reason to declare themselves free from such tyranny.

Today we have been asleep to the enemies of freedom for all. Monopolies both public and private tend toward tyranny and must be changed with the grace of God. The wholesale assault on godly living and protection of evil has many of us crying out to God for His Day of Vengeance to comfort all who mourn (Isaiah 61:2). It might be well to fasten this firmly in our minds and pray for the grace to believe this completely: God has rules that aren't suggestions but commandments, and they are for our good, both now and through eternity. The fear of God isn't a fear to come to Him or stay close to Him but a fear of departing from Him.

South of Carmel, California, is a gorgeous coastline with a winding road cut into the cliffs. The view is so beautiful as long as you stay on the road! Everyone has a fear of going over the cliffs by departing from the road. This illustration is similar to our walk with God: be afraid to depart from God but not to enjoy Him.

Jeremiah's prophecies were used by Daniel to start praying to end the first captivity of Judah, because Jeremiah had said the captivity would only last seventy years.

Today Jeremiah records God's promise to show us great and mighty things that we don't know (Jeremiah 33:3). Jeremiah continues on through this chapter foretelling God healing Israel, curing them (probably from the jab) and giving them abundance of peace; then goes on to describe Israel's population returning from all nations and God building them just as He did when Israel first started in the land. God goes on to describe salvation in Christ by cleansing and forgiving them from all their sins. Verse nine describes how God gets worldwide glory from doing this: "And it shall be to me a name of joy, a praise and honor before all nations of the earth, which shall hear all the good that I do unto them: and they shall fear and tremble for all the goodness and all the prosperity that I procure unto it." The chapter goes on and says David will be king and will execute judgment and righteousness in the land, so much so that Jerusalem will be called "The LORD our righteousness." Then God goes on by taking an oath to establish David and his descendants and the Levites and all Israel by twice taking an oath.

Allowing the Scriptures to speak for themselves isn't easy if we have been sitting under theological teachers and not in the whole Bible for ourselves. Most Christians have heard Christ instructing them as they read the Scriptures. It's as if the words are jumping off the page. Jesus declared He would be our teacher, so it only makes sense to call no man our teacher, since in Matthew 23:8 Christ commands to call no man our teacher. The Scriptures are simple to understand with the Author, if we have faith to believe them and enter into the promises: Jesus is the Author of that faith. I'm going to outline the simple steps the Scriptures invite us to enter into to obtain the promises already given us.

The principles laid out in this book have succeeded every single time they have been tried over the entire span of human history. The promises made to Israel at this time in history have been sealed with many oaths made by Almighty God. Not only will we see the stopping of the great reset, we will see the reversal of tyrannical control over man. How am I so sure of this? Over the next few chapters, you'll see my journey through the Scriptures with its Author and see as I did the simple, unavoidable Truth.

Jesus is the author and finisher of our faith. Heb 12:2. Believing his words are extremely important and not believing them is calling God a liar. John 3:33. This faith can't be produced humanly but only we can come to God for it. We can even see this great sin of lack of faith in ourselves or others and call for God to restore what is missing. I John 5:15–16.

We must pray like never before for everything lacking and cast every care upon him!

Hebrews 11:6 but without faith it is impossible to please him for he that cometh to God must believe that He is, and He is a rewarder of them that diligently seek Him.

# CHAPTER 2

# THE MYSTERY OF THE MISSING SEVEN WEEKS OF DANIEL

The personal involvement of God in the world's daily affairs has been set aside almost entirely by modern-day end-times preaching, and a fatalistic sinking-ship theory has taken its place since D. L. Moody. Naturally this fatalism led them to call Hitler the antichrist and sensationalize many events as the end of the world and the immanent rapture of the church, with much debate as to the rapture's timing in relation to the 70th week of Daniel's great tribulation. This theological exercise pressed forward without any serious regard to the hundreds of scriptures related to all Israel needing to be saved with David as king and the kingdom restored to Israel, as clearly stated in Hosea 3:4–5. 4. For the children of Israel shall abide many days without a king and without a prince, and without a sacrifice... 5. Afterwards, shall the children of Israel return, and seek the Lord their God, and David their king; and shall fear the Lord and His Goodness in the latter days.

Probably the most pointed experience I've ever had that God Himself had been involved in America's founding and was actively defending and perfecting us was while evangelizing at our local truck stop. It was a good evening with two teams of two going from truck to truck. Jason was preaching quite forcefully to a couple of truckers from Columbia, with the one in the driver's seat throwing out insults against America and God between Jason's good preaching. Somehow the man's hatred for God and America was coupled together.

Jason preached on in wonderful power from the Holy Spirit when the man became extremely nervous and started blurting out repeatedly, "I'm a good person." I felt pushed forward by God, and I forcefully stated that I took issue with him calling himself a good person when he had just denied his Maker and slammed America. I asked him, if the Communists in Venezuela came and invaded his country, who would they call to help them? He sheepishly admitted the USA. Jason briefly preached a bit more, ending with telling them that Christ said, "If you are ashamed of Me, I will be ashamed of you." Then Jason headed to the next truck. I stepped forward and handed the truckers a pocket New Testament, which the driver promptly threw across the cab. I followed Jason to the last of the trucks, then what happened next amazed us.

While waiting inside the truck stop, this Columbian truck driver and his partner came inside looking for Jason. They approached Jason from the back and clutched Jason's arm, saying, "We need to receive Christ right now. We've seen all the angels." Jason's first thought was that he was being mocked, but when he turned and saw the man's face, he was crying, and his partner was bawling. Two broken men wanting to be saved. Jason prayed with them right there in the truck stop. The driver raised his hands in the air and said, "I love the USA!" Then they desperately wanted to know how to stay close to God. Jason told them to read the New Testament we had given them, then promptly went to his car to give them his own full Bible.

Jason's curiosity couldn't hold back any longer, so he asked, "What do you mean you've seen all the angels?" The driver asked, "Didn't you see them?" Jason was oblivious but thought they must have seen something when the driver kept blurting, "I'm a good person." The men related how they had both seen angels standing behind us, and one had a purple sash across his chest and a rainbow for a crown. As we walked away, the angels followed us, and the last one with a rainbow crown spoke to him in a voice that pierced right into him but not through his ears: "Now do you believe?" The two men were stunned and thought that it was a hallucination until they compared what they saw. Then they were more afraid. The driver asked the other man to pick up the Bible he had thrown across the cab, but he said, "No, it's open. We should read a verse that it's open to." So he carefully picked up the Bible and read the first verse he glanced at: "If you are ashamed of me, I will be ashamed of you." Jason's last words to them. They then went searching for Jason.

When we read Daniel, chapter 9, the reward to Daniel for being faithful to God was to explain the future of God's working with the nation Israel. The seventy weeks of Israel's history is at the centerpiece of this reward. We might look at our own reward from God to understand the simplicity of this prophecy because it's at the heart of what's going on today.

Our university system has been taken over by left-wing thinkers, and our seminaries haven't been exempt. But even before the massive push from the left in our seminaries, the mystery of the language used in describing sixty-nine of those seventy weeks has been debated for centuries. Even Sir Isaac Newton weighed in an opinion about this confusing text that actually is quite simple and proves what a literary genius our Lord is.

Back in 2017, the Lord specifically told me one day to read the passage in Daniel about the seventy weeks of Daniel. I really didn't think that unusual at first because of the multiple times He has spoken to me to read a scripture. Yet I was intrigued, because maybe it held a key to something that had bothered me for about a decade. That bothersome thing started shortly after I was granted a miracle almost instantly after I prayed in 2005 for Him to sell a house that was frankly my dream project and that was way out of reach for most buyers. After weeks of nonstop open houses, my prayer was really simple: "Lord, if You sell this house this weekend, I will serve You, and You will not be disappointed!" Five minutes later, a lady walked in and said, "This is my house!" She hadn't even gotten past the great room.

So the first order of spiritual business was a very direct command to read ten pages a day out of my Bible. My Bible is large-print, old King James Version, with a margin on both sides of each page for notes and cross references in the middle column: 1,341 pages of Old and New Testament, or 134 days. Wow, I would read the Bible about two and a half times a year. *I'm really going to be smart* was my first thought, which was instantly revised by God: *No, you will be very humbled and able to hear My voice clearly.*

That bothersome thing was really huge. It was born out of reading my Bible from cover to cover over 8 times, and about the same for the New Testament separately. That huge thing was the spiritual and physical restoration of Israel. It wouldn't have been huge at all if people were talking about it, but they weren't, at least in any circle of Christians I knew. Complete silence was as close as I can describe it. Various explanations were given, such as, "It's just pictorial language describing something else." So I start posing questions to the best scholars in the group: If the valley of dry bones in Ezekiel 37 isn't literally dry bones coming together, with cartilage, muscles, and skin put on them when God breathes on them; then they stand to their feet, an exceedingly great army that was slain and that is the whole house of Israel, then how could God have phrased it differently that you could take it literally? This didn't seem to faze them; they just simply said no: as in no way can they believe it. Faith is truly a gift from the Author and finisher of our faith. Never hesitate to ask for more faith if you need it.

I obediently went to the prophecy in Daniel and read it just as God had told me. He said, read it again; then, on the third time through, it seemed maybe that the seven weeks mentioned was the great restoration of Israel that was so prominent in Scripture. The fourth command to read it again was really exciting. I felt like enlightenment and understanding was generating inside me. Wow. Of course, there are two commands to rebuild Jerusalem and two comings of the same Messiah sandwiched into one verse. The first command was by Cyrus, and the second command to rebuild Jerusalem was by God Himself. Then the first coming was Christ dying for our sins, and in the second Christ gathers His own at the rapture. Let's see if you can see it:

> Know therefore and understand, that from the going forth of the commandment to restore and rebuild Jerusalem unto the Messiah the Prince shall be 7 weeks and 62 weeks… And after 62 weeks shall the Messiah be cut off, but not for Himself… (Daniel 9:25–26)

This was fantastic. It all fit together, especially with the parable of the fig tree, where Jesus said a dormant fig tree planted in the land would come to life and that generation would not pass away until all things be fulfilled. I just assumed this would fit perfectly with respected theology dates, or so I thought. Man, was I naive: I found a wide range of dates from all sorts of sources, but I couldn't find any that took the date of King Cyrus's command to restore and rebuild Jerusalem and add 62 weeks, or 434 years, which is 7 times 62. I was so confused I had no idea what to do. I prayed, and instantly the Lord said, "Look for dates that would pinpoint it indirectly."

I turned to my Jewish calendar (Chabad.org). It also had important Jewish dates in history. Jackpot: the death of Nebuchadnezzar in 397BC. So add 62 weeks, and bingo: AD 37. Oh, a little history lesson out of the book of Daniel chapter 5: The death of Nebuchadnezzar instated his son Belshazzar, which probably from the text reigned just a bit over two years until replaced by the Medes (King Darius) and the Persians (King Cyrus). Cyrus made the command in the first year of his reign to restore and rebuild Jerusalem in Ezra, chapter 1. So probably around AD 39, the 434 years pinpoints the death of Christ. And about 31 years later is AD 70, where not one stone is left upon another, as Christ had said. When the Romans attacked in AD 70, the Jews ran into the temple to hide. The Romans burned the temple and the gold ran down in between the stones, and they dismantled it for the gold. Just as Jesus had said. I turned to a well-documented historical fact of AD 70, the destruction of Jerusalem, so some fraudster couldn't simply add in those missing seven weeks of Daniel (forty-nine years) because that would put it well beyond AD 70.

Another pinpointing from the Jewish calendar is the dedication of the second temple in 349 BC, which gives them about 46 years to complete the temple from Cyrus's decree, which is about the time it took to build Herod's temple a few centuries later. Its dedication is in Ezra, chapter 6. This bit of history is extremely important to destroying the modern-day dates that result from adding the 62 weeks together with the 7 weeks (483 years), because if there's an additional 49 years, it would have taken 95 years to build the temple. This would have been impossible since all of the original builders, like Nehemiah and Ezra, were at the dedication. Truth has a way of proving that things don't add up for the unbelievers' spin on the truth.

Understanding this missing seven weeks of Daniel will clarify most all of the parables and predictions by Christ in the New Testament and fit them together with the massive amount of scripture in the Old Testament. This will end the debate as to when the Messiah (Jesus Christ) will appear in the clouds to rapture His church of true believers, not the day or the hour but a very close time frame: forty-nine years after God makes His decree to rebuild and restore Jerusalem. Just before the massive attack on Israel in Ezekiel 38, there is an earthquake that destroys Jerusalem. With the current sentiments in Israel to preserve everything old, this earthquake is a huge time-saver, so everything needs to be rebuilt.

Massive deception has clouded the dating of this prophecy, but what's to be gained by this? Maybe the "great reset," because if churchgoers were expecting the rapture without Israel's complete physical and spiritual restoration, they would be lulled to sleep, thinking this is just God's plan and the one world government that the Book of Revelations and the seventieth week of Daniel predict. In reality, we're seeing a last great attempt to set up one world government before Israel comes to faith in Christ and the kingdom is returned to Israel, just as was the last question the disciples asked Jesus before He ascended into heaven in a cloud. Satanic forces have been attempting one world government since the Tower of Babel, and Rome was trying to do just that during the time Jesus walked the earth. God flipped those plans upside down by the conversion of Constantine, and the whole Roman Empire was affected by Christians. I'm expecting a similar flip at God's day of vengeance on the wicked to comfort all who mourn (Isaiah 61:2, Jeremiah 30:23–24).

The plans for this great reset have been in the making for over a hundred years and involve many of the most powerful people in the world, but that's nothing new. Hitler and the Third Reich, Communists, and now this. When we believe Scripture, certain things must happen first, and certain foretold attitudes and events will proceed the rapture of the church. After God's command to rebuild and restore Jerusalem (Ezekiel 37:26–28), the approximate time of the rapture will be clear, seven weeks or forty-nine years. Not the day or the hour, as Christ clearly stated, but a close time that would send people out to meet the Lord as in the parable of the ten virgins, which explains Jesus's teaching that people should not be going on as usual as in the days of Noah: eating, drinking, marrying and giving in marriage, right up until Noah entered the ark.

A good list of events that will take place prior to the rapture might tend to distract people from what's happening now in God's Kingdom and our role as Christians in this very important next event that will literally change the world for Good. But the most obvious event from 1 Thessalonians is that it will be a time of peace and safety. We have everything but peace and safety now. In the addendum, I put together a chronology of events from now, through the spiritual and physical restoration of Israel, to the revealing of the antichrist, then the rapture of the church before the great tribulation, the best I could.

# CHAPTER 3

# VENGEANCE IS MINE, SAYS THE LORD

We have been bombarded with so much "tolerance" in today's world and churchianity that it's a foreign concept to us that God would ever take vengeance. About a decade ago, I was parking my car full of grandkids and snow equipment at our Tehachapi Mountain park, when I noticed a carload of young Muslims unloading for the same fun purpose. I prayed to be able to talk with them, but it wasn't working out. After a few hours of fun sliding down the mountain, we started the hike back to the SUV. My prayer was answered as our trail converged with the five Muslim kids.

I asked if their god forgave sin. Their reply was very respectful and had a great respect for their religion. Basically forgiveness was based on confession of the sin and not doing it again. I wanted to make sure I hadn't missed anything, so I asked, "Is that all?" They looked at each other as if to double-check that nothing was left out and answered, "Yes, that's it." So I simply replied, "If that's really all there is to it, then (I used the name of their god) is an unjust god." The girls gasped and put their hands on their mouths, and the boys' veins on their necks popped out as they took a defensive pose. I stood there and looked as innocent and puzzled as I could. Then one asked, "Doesn't your God forgive sin?" I didn't know the answer to this question would have so much intrigue to them, but it really drew them into deep thought. My reply was simply, "Not until He takes vengeance against that sin. In the case of man's sins, the price is death, so God so loved us that He sent His only Son to die and put our sins on His Son." Their reply was in unison: "Do you have a Bible we can have?"

A sense of justice is one of the strongest senses inside every human being. Years of Hollywood movies have conditioned us that we can't stand the thought of the bad guy getting away, and we even want the good guy to kill him.

There's another conditioning that has invaded our thinking from mostly media and entertainment sources: tolerance. Tolerance is a wonderful thing if it's godly tolerance, such as with race issues. But when it crosses the line that Martin Luther King set, we're in trouble. He dreamed of a day that we would not be judged by the color of our skin but by the measure of our character. "Godliness exalts a nation, but sin is a reproach to any people" (Proverbs 14:34). Tolerance of molesters of children is evil in itself, as is tolerance of murderers of babies, and a host of other evils that we are told to tolerate by the most vile people that have ever walked the face of the earth.

Jesus told a parable in Luke 18:1–8 with a refreshing ending. The parable tells of a widow with an enemy. She pesters a judge until he avenged her of her enemy. Jesus uses this parable to illustrate how much more our Heavenly Father will avenge His elect who cry day and night unto Him. There's never been a time more than now when America needed to be avenged by The Father Himself of our enemies. It would appear this parable was written specifically for us Christians now, because Jesus says as a conclusion to this parable and promise, "But nevertheless, will the Son of Man find faith on the earth when He returns?" The parable in Luke 18 is preceded by Jesus talking of the end times, teaching us to be ready spiritually, which makes Jesus's parable even more applicable for today. The left are going after our children and grandchildren. Jesus promises that if we knock, the door will open; if we ask, we will receive; and if we seek, we will find. God is personal; not a god that is far off. In fact, He is looking for hearts that are perfect toward Him, so that He can show Himself strong unto them (2 Chronicles 16:9).

Jesus warned of hell more than He talked about Heaven. He made a host of enemies in the religious community. To have this Jesus rebranded as a quiet, mild-mannered man is the exact opposite of reality. Sounds like the work of the leftist propaganda machine to me. I believe we would be shocked to know how few pulpit preachers have ever read the Bible cover to cover. The lie that it takes an expert to read and understand the Scriptures isn't what Christ said. How about this one: "Call no man your teacher, for one is your teacher, even Christ." Or in Luke 18:17: "Unless you become like little children you shall not enter the kingdom of God." This verse puts a requirement on us to be yoked together with Christ to learn of Him: Matthew 11:28–29.

Our understanding of vengeance and justice has been dulled by this constant rebranding of the Christ of the Bible. Few talk about looking at porn as an offense that will get you into hell, but that's squarely what Jesus taught in Matthew 5:27–32. If you looked up those verses, you probably noticed that divorce was also given some strict parameters that aren't typically taught today. Remarriages to divorced women were labeled as adultery for all parties mentioned. Isn't it interesting that a perfect description of our typical pulpit occupiers is found in Jesus's half brother's book, Jude 4? "For there are certain men crept in unawares, which were before ordained to this condemnation, ungodly men, turning the Grace of our God into lasciviousness [shameless immortality]…"

God's pretty heavy on judgment, but we can avert those judgments and get God on our side by turning to Him for help. There are thousands of scriptures where God promises judgment, and even one that promises that judgment must begin at the household of God. I'm convinced we aren't going to change church without at least some of the judgments promised to the leadership in our churches taking place. We see a host of wrathful dictators making the entire world take a very questionable shot in the arm, even for five-year-olds. They are flexing their muscles, but with massive resistance. Yet for the most part our pulpits are filled with men who have no idea what to do and are oftentimes afraid to take any side at all. When abortion topics were raging, the same fence-sitting pulpit cowards were able to make themselves look good while millions of innocents were led to their slaughter. There's never a substitute for courage, and there's no better courage than what God Himself offers.

Take David, for example. There's a boy who became a man through adversity. If it hadn't been for the adversities, we would see a far different David. David's psalms are full of complaints against his enemies, but as David focused on God Himself, there's an interesting perspective adjustment that takes place. Faith in the promises of God turns to faith in God Himself for everything; from direction from God Himself, to courage to face His enemies, to certainty that God Himself would go with him to strengthen David and fight with David and for David. This crying out for help is the only reasonable response to our God who has made so many promises to us.

# CHANGING WHO WE ARE

In 1969, I was my own worst enemy, and it seemed if it could go wrong, it did. I couldn't really stand myself. I was selfish and a liar and into the sins of the sixties. I thought changing myself would be simple, so I set out to do just that, but the harder I tried the worse I got. I was a slave trapped in my own selfish body.

The year 1970 came, and I turned twenty-one. It looked like I was going to break my declaration to my fraternity brothers that I would stop going to bars when I turned twenty-one because it wouldn't be any fun if it were legal. I picked up a girl hitchhiking in the Santa Cruz mountains and asked her for a fun place to go. She immediately said Koinonia House. I listened to the directions but was too messed up to possibly remember how to get there. When she got out of the car, it was as if her words were guiding me right to the place. It felt good but really unusual.

I was starving, but bars didn't have good food, so I looked around for a restaurant. There was nothing, so I just went in to the place anyway. To my pleasant surprise, it was a café that had wonderful food. It was run entirely by young people like myself. The girls were different, with an inner glow that was really attractive in the purest way possible. A guy came and talked to me about Christ and how Jesus had done so much for him in Vietnam. But the girls were shining from their whole being that God loved everyone. Maybe for the first time in years, I had hope and I started loving people too in small ways.

About two weeks later, I was at the lowest spot ever: all engineered by God. After a night of barhopping and comparing the bar women to the wonderful girls at the café, I lay down to sleep. About 2:00 a.m., I saw a vision of myself walking into a room. A television was on, and Billy Graham was yelling really loud, "Ask Christ into your life, and He will change your life." That was the end of the vision. I was shocked and felt urged by God to do that very thing: to ask Christ into my life. But in classic sinner style, I replied, "I don't need to do that." Then a clear voice came to me and said, "Try it. You have tried everything else." I hadn't a clue who was talking to me, but he knew me very well. So I said, "Jesus, if You're real, come into my life."

The most powerful and loving and holy person came right into me. I instantly started repenting of all the bad things I had done. As I finished one thing, the next was brought to my remembrance. It took a long time to do this. But when I finally got to the end of the list, I felt horrible. I was shown that because of a black sin nature inside me about the size of my fist, I would go do these sins again. I was horrified and couldn't think of anything worse. I cried out, "Father, take this thing away. I don't want to sin anymore. I want to live for You."

Instantly, I was taken to a pitch-black place with no light except on a post in front of me as I was kneeling there. I knew it was a very important place but couldn't understand why there was a large post in front of me. I started looking up the post, and as I did so, I was taken up, and I was looking at Christ hanging on the cross, bloody and beaten, yet still alive. He looked at me and somehow loved me with His gaze. I was standing now and noticed a bright light far away to my right. It was the arm of the Father. I somehow knew that. It was heading straight for me, and His hand reached inside me and grasped my sin factory, as I called it, and then like a baseball pitcher threw my sin nature on His only Son. It hit Him right in the same spot that it was taken out of me, center chest. Jesus winced in pain as it hit Him. Suddenly, I was standing next to the old dead me on my right and Christ dying on my left. The whole thing of Christ's death made total sense. And as fast as I was transported to Jerusalem almost two thousand years ago, I was transported back. I jumped to my feet in those precious predawn hours and yelled, "That's why You died!"

My life changed instantly. My friends took less than twenty seconds to notice, and, after a few weeks, I started to read the Bible. I couldn't believe how alive the book was and how the words jumped off the page into my heart. The Word, as the Bible refers to Christ in John chapter 1, did further refinement of my attitudes toward everything. Sometimes I would find myself at odds with the Bible, but help was only a sincere prayer away, such as one I prayed: "Lord, I know Your Word says this very plainly, but it doesn't seem right to me. Would You help me to believe Your Word?" Within seconds, the answer came, complete with illustrations and examples from Scripture and with a heart to believe it. It seems the more of the Scriptures I know, the easier it is for God to correct or teach me.

Discipline from God is truly some of the most precious times in my life. The Bible says if we're without discipline, we're bastards, not sons. I even shortly after my born-again experience prayed for discipline to keep me close to Him. David had a departure-from-God experience that was so severe, and that he was so blind, that God sent Nathan the prophet to convict him by trapping him to condemn himself. The story is in 2 Samuel, which is the life of David as king. His repentance of this great sin is in Psalms 51. David doesn't attempt to change himself but depends entirely on God to change him in every way, including restoring of the joy of his salvation. Then David gave himself a job, much like the one Christ has left with us: tell others about Him.

Our attitudes are so important to God because they direct our future actions, as I learned in 1979, when we were obeying God's direction to leave Orange County and move to Tehachapi. We had purchased a small acreage dependent on the sale of our house in Orange County. I got so sick I really believed I was going to die, so I cried out to the Father, asking Him what was wrong. The answer was instant and pierced my heart: "You're coveting the money you're getting from this house." I replied, "You're so right! The best I can, I give it all to You." God's answer was instant. I was taken in a vision to the acreage we had planned to build on, and as I looked at it from a distance, a house came down from the sky and was placed on the property. I felt so good with such confirmation that God's help would be with every detail of our move and project. Then I noticed that I was no longer sick, even in the least. Giving ourselves and all we have to God is no small thing, and as Christ's words pierce our hearts, obedience brings much reward that repositions our lives as God's children in His plans, not merely as students but learning by being yoked together with Christ as our life source.

Listen to Christ's words as He talks with His disciples before His death: "I am the vine, ye are the branches; he that abideth in Me, and I in him, the same bringeth forth much fruit: for without Me ye can do nothing" (John 15:5).

The streets in Los Angeles skid row might have the highest density of hopeless people. I was amazed how, without fail, their knowledge of the good news or gospel, as it's called, was so incomplete that it would not be an exaggeration in my mind that they had never heard enough of the gospel to actually change their life since there was a mixture of mostly self-effort. Most felt so condemned from their lack of self-discipline to rid themselves of drugs or alcohol that the only escape from that condemnation was more drugs or alcohol. I would often start my conversation with, "You know there's only One Savior from sin, and it isn't you or me." The reactions were pretty consistent: they had never heard that before. What a relief to finally hear Christ's words, that if the Son shall set you free, you shall be free indeed. The Gospel is simple: We come to Christ and do the admitting of all our sins as His spotlight of truth shines in our hearts, and then at our request, He makes us new creatures in CHRIST!

What a relief it was for me that Christ would set me free from sin when I first met Him. Drugs, alcohol, and every other lust were instantly taken away, and a love for God and all things godly put in its place.

Then much later, I experienced the shame and condemnation that resulted after being born again, then being ensnared again in sin, which was really just my own self-righteous thinking that I could keep myself just. Paul tried the same approach in Romans chapter 7.

It seems as if God would let me fail a thousand times if that's what it took to realize, like Paul, that Jesus Christ delivers instantly from sin, while my own power was totally powerless. Much like Acts 4:12: "There is no other name given amongst men whereby we must be saved." Skid row or the nearby glass skyscrapers, the need for Christ is exactly the same. The removal of a basically selfish nature, and being given a new selfless nature, is something only Christ can do. Second Corinthians 5–17 to the end of the chapter is great reading.

One of my favorite stories was told to me by Lisa, a fellow evangelist, while evangelizing at a bus station with a bar next to it in a rather shabby part of the city. She approached a man sitting alone drinking a beer and asked him to receive Christ as Lord and Savior. His reply was he had lost everything in the last two weeks: a hundred-thousand-dollar job, wife, kids, house, and expensive SUV. Lisa's reply was, "That's wonderful!" His reply was, "Are you crazy, woman?" Lisa said, "No, because if you still had all those things, you wouldn't even listen to me." He admitted she was right, and after he had received Christ and repented of his sins, he thanked God he allowed him to lose everything to receive him.

# CHAPTER 5

# Thy Will Be Done on Earth as It Is in Heaven

It's been a great revelation to me that all our problems in the world are a direct result of rebellion against God. Jesus's disciples were wanting to know how to pray. It was a completely open-ended question. Jesus starts by stating, "Our Father, which art in heaven." Notice that it's "Our Father," as for a group of disciples. That same "Our" continues throughout the prayer; not singular prayer life but one that recognizes the need for the whole to be engaged. Jesus tells us that His Father is also our Father. This moves us close to Him and Him close to us. Not a dictator, but Our Father.

Jesus continues: "Hallowed be Thy name." Perhaps for today, this is the most needful ingredient in our prayers. Taking God for granted or as a buddy, or the other extreme, seeing Him being unapproachable: either way, it twists the truth and keeps the powerful, loving, and holy God from becoming what He desires. Holiness is the primary essence of God. His name is not to be marginalized, or worse. With kings, we see the kings' servants oftentimes saying, "In the name of the king." It extends the kingdom of the king to wherever His faithful servants are. Power by proxy, we might say, for earthly kings. But in our case, Jesus declares, "The kingdom of God is within you." This close personal relationship with our Father in heaven is based on our righteousness being of God. Walking in the light as He is in the light, the Blood of Jesus Christ His Son cleansing us from all sin, and confessing our sins and being cleansed from all unrighteousness (notice that word *all*) (1 John 1:7–10).

Jesus declares in John chapter 10, that His sheep hear His voice and they follow Him. There's a holy walk with our Holy God. Hypocrisy separates us from all the privileges of being the King's child, such as whatsoever we ask in Jesus's name, He will do. A wealthy Father wants to give to His children, especially things like wisdom, righteousness, faith, and courage. Our Father is giving us the most priceless thing in the universe: His character.

"Thy kingdom come, Thy will be done on earth as it is in heaven." This scripture is so overlooked, and we rob ourselves and our children by not taking it seriously. Think of heaven: does anybody dare sin or encourage others that it's okay to sin in the very presence of God? The most natural response to meeting God is to thoroughly repent of our sins, so the presence of God is everywhere, abiding in us, with righteousness and true justice reigning everywhere. Nations that are under God with rulers who fear God, not the media, the FBI, the unions, the great reset but God Himself. Abortion would be no more, divorces would nearly cease, cremation would be abhorrent, homosexuality would be a great shame, children would be highly valuable, and all forms of abuse would cease. The wealth of the average person would increase, and monopolies would disappear, both public and private. A man could support his family with an average job, and righteousness would flood the land, along with peace and healthy people. Fear of lying or any form of corruption would guide every individual. A husband and wife were struck dead for lying in the early church. Great fear came over the whole church. Americans should have that same fear as we are one nation under God.

Notice that the will of God being done on earth as it is in heaven is the first request for us.

The next request for us is: "Give us this day our daily bread. And forgive us our debts as we forgive our debtors. And lead us not into temptation but deliver us from evil." These words are grouped together for a reason. The next part gives us the why: "For Thine is the kingdom, and the power, and the glory forever. Amen." Forgiveness from God is essential when we repent of our sins, and it demands we do the same for our fellow man. Entering God's kingdom in this life puts all the responsibilities of daily life on our King, and our only focus need be on obedience to Him.

Everything good is from God and powered by Him, and He wants us to be part of that. His kingdom is the natural part of inviting Him to rule over us. Therefore, it's very important for us to do that as individuals and read the Bible for ourselves. People who believe the Bible is confusing and requires some theology to interpret it haven't met Christ in the Scriptures yet: The words aren't jumping off the page, and the Author isn't there giving them life. This is not to say you'll understand everything, but you will have confidence that eventually you will know even as you're known by God. These words will never pass away, but heaven and earth will.

Crying out for God's kingdom is as natural for a child of God as any other need they have. That inner yearning for righteousness to rule and corruption to cease is in every child of the King, and this book is written so that every reader will be revived to cry out to the Father to bring His kingdom on earth as it is in heaven.

Bitterness toward God is often caused by some great loss of something God gave us. Bitterness short-circuits our prayer life first, then moves us to unbelief. In street evangelism, encountering bitterness is more common than you might think, but it takes being willing to listen to really help people.

A few years back, when planning a trip to the local community college, the Lord plainly said to me, "I want you to go to the bus station too." This direction to also go to the bus station too came several times. Then while at the college, that small, still voice said, "Drop everything and go to the bus station now." We showed up at the station and were talking to a man when a woman showed up about thirty feet away. The Lord said, "Go talk to her," so we excused ourselves and started walking toward her with our New Testaments in our hands. She started yelling at us as we neared fifteen feet away:

"You don't want to talk to me. I don't believe a word of it." So I kept coming with full knowledge that God wanted me to talk to her.

Smiling, I asked her why she didn't believe a word of the Bible. She said that even though she was raised in church, her baby girl had died a few years ago. I sympathized with her, then, getting my words from Christ, asked her, where does she think her little girl is right now? She replied with broken speech, "I hope she's in heaven with God." I said, "That's exactly right; she was totally innocent and she's there right now." Then I asked, "What do you think she's doing right now?" She burst into tears so much that the sidewalk became wet. It took her a few moments to answer, and when she did, she spoke very brokenly and could barely get out the words: "She's praying for me!"

Yes, what a divine revelation for that broken woman. She was overjoyed and even started preaching to us. I shared how the Lord had directed us to the bus station for that moment, and then she shared how she was a registered nurse and owned a car but for some reason wanted to take the bus! Such rejoicing in heaven and on earth. Others can be defiled by letting bitterness take root in our lives, the Scriptures say; but so many can be healed by Jesus binding up the brokenhearted as He was sent to do (Isaiah 61:1–2).

# CHAPTER 6

# HAS THE WORLD GONE INSANE?

It would seem that way since 2020 to me and to many others. A "plandemic" over a virus that had about a 99.98 percent recovery rate! That is a two out of ten thousand death rate. Lockdowns, travel restrictions, business and whole county closures, and masks upon masks. We played along for about three days, then invited our neighbors over for dinner. At that early stage, few knew anything, but I knew what liars the mainstream media is. The hype was so similar to the "orange man bad" routine that had permeated their worldwide network monopolies of phony news stories for the past four years. Twitter files and Tucker expose the CIA and FBI for what they truly are. The deep state in conjunction with monopolistic businesses and foreign bad actors has shown its true intentions to bury us in my opinion.

Mail in ballots have been a huge goal of the plandemic, making election fraud by electronic means covered up by phony paper ballots. I may be a pessimist in the ability of fixing this thing being humanly possible, but it seems obvious to me we need the help and intervention of the God of the Bible. We wrestle not against flesh and blood but against spiritual powers and wickedness in high places (Ephesians 6). We were never created to be self-sufficient. Adam walked with God before the fall of man. David became a man after God's own heart.

Spring is my favorite time of year, especially after a long dry autumn and a harsh winter. Warmer sunshine days, and everything turning a soft green with colorful splashes of color carpeting the hills. Everything seems like it's been waiting to spring forth, to burst into its most beautiful state. The same is true with the animal kingdom as well as with us humans. Wedding bells ring; children sing as if we all had wings. God's creation was God's gift to mankind, but it was never designed to be without God Himself. Jesus came to reveal His Father to us. In John 14, Jesus said, "If you've seen Me, you've seen the Father." Imagine being blind, and Jesus makes you see; or being lame, unable to walk, and Jesus makes you able to run and leap; or being covered in sores that are consuming your body, and Jesus touches you and makes your skin perfect again. Much like spring is to our natural world, Jesus makes a new physical world for our necessities, and even beyond that, He cleans the vileness of this selfish, evil world from our hearts and makes us new creatures with clean hearts with the purest of motives. This is the spring that Christ gives us is forever, not just every April, May, and June.

Blasting around the earth in our outer sphere went China's hypersonic vehicle, nuclear-capable and untouchable by our defenses, threatening the earth with nuclear winter. Nefarious actors threaten to enslave and unleash bio-weapons on the masses. Religious fanatics near possession of nuclear weapons. Sea levels supposedly rising seem rather mild to the other MANufactured crises.

The contrast between God's spring and man's worldwide self-destruction is stark. Man without God vs. man with God. Man against God vs. God with man. This might seem too simplistic to most people. Most are thinking this is more complex than God vs. the devil. So it would seem to many and especially the religious seminary type: thinking of free will of man, or God being so sovereign that we can't influence Him at all. Well, let me tackle both of these naysayers, and not so much for the purpose of convincing a single one of them but for the open-to-God's-Word believers.

God's Word talks of several things happening in the latter days. Since God cannot lie, and not a single scripture was broken in Jesus's first coming, it should be safe to say that the same will apply toward Christ's second coming.

Let's get started with the basics that have yet to be fulfilled:

- Judgment of the shepherds (Ezekiel 34 and Jeremiah 25)
- Day of vengeance on the wicked (Isaiah 61:2, Jeremiah 30:23–24)
- David reigns as king of Israel (Ezekiel 34 and 37, Hosea 3, Jeremiah 30:9)
- Israel attacked by a multitude of nations, and God defends them supernaturally (Ezekiel 38–39)
- Israel and America avenged of their common enemies (Ezekiel 35 and specifically verses 9–12)
- All Israel is saved (Romans 11, Ezekiel 36 and 39, Jeremiah 31)
- Jesus's parable of the fig tree in Matthew, Mark, and Luke
- Physical restoration of Jerusalem, and temple built with stream from the altar healing the Dead Sea; Israel massively expands its borders apparantly without war (Jeremiah 31, Ezekiel 40–48)

This massive expansion of Israel seems to be without war, but remember David rules as king and many nations are marveling and fearing what God is doing for Israel. Ezekiel 35:10–11 clearly states God has two nations, two nations with a common enemy (Islam hates the USA and Israel). America's the Israel of the West and along with Israel will be revived when those nations that hate us are judged. "I will make Myself known among them, when I have judged thee" (Ezekiel 35:11). In Ezekiel 38–39, we see that promised judgment.

These are just a few of the many things that have to come to pass before the rapture of the church. Most theological positions either ignore these passages or move them to after the great tribulation during the thousand-year reign of Christ; or dismiss them as Israel being too hard-hearted toward Christ and has thrown away this great opportunity to be restored. None of these excuses hold water, if they know the Scriptures. First objection is easy to destroy: How is David king when Jesus is the King of kings and sits on David's throne? The second one is even easier to debunk: God takes their heart of stone out of them and replaces it with a heart of flesh (Ezekiel 36:26). So what these theologians teach as a disqualification because Israel is too hard-hearted is actually the prophecy qualification.

Theology has over forty-five thousand different versions to it, which is rivaling the number of verses in the entire Bible. It's been said: a theologian is a person who can take something relatively simple and make it so complex you can't understand it anymore. Charles Finney is one of my favorite evangelists, but he seemed to lose his anointing as he became a theologian. His focus on repentance and world-changing revival switched to mentally interesting topics that ceased to bring revival to all. The apostle Paul has some of the most insightful verses in chapters 9–11 of Romans. He had no problem teaching God's sovereignty alongside human responsibility, but he didn't pretend to necessarily have a complete understanding of it as he nears the end of chapter 11 and declares this in verse 33: "Oh, the depth of the riches both of the wisdom and knowledge of God! how unsearchable are His judgements, and His ways past finding out!" So this conclusion doesn't lead Paul to a theology to answer his questions, rather Paul makes this logical conclusion in the first two verses of the next chapter:

> I beseech you therefore, brethren by the mercies of God, that ye present your bodies a living sacrifice, holy, acceptable unto God, which is your reasonable service. And be not conformed to this world: but be ye transformed by the renewing of your mind, that you may prove what is that good, and acceptable, and perfect will of God.

Our reading of Scripture, or listening to preaching or teaching or Christian music, should draw us into this closer walk with Christ.

When a true believer talks about the Word, he often pounds on his chest to indicate where that Word abides, not on his head as if it were merely interesting or inspiring. The Word is transformational because it is alive and powerful and sharper than a two-edged sword dividing between the soul and the spirit. Hebrews 4:12 has this text, but the entire chapter is fantastic. Our soul contains our emotions and is a wonderful thing in the saved man, but it's not a good leader of our lives; the spirit is for that. We have a prison in our town, and we could install a sign over its entrance saying, "These inmates followed their emotions and ended up here." We must be born again and have a soul saved from envy, hate, jealousy, and selfish desires, and only the Word of God can separate our emotions from the Spirit so we can be Spirit-led.

So in conclusion, theology tends to make us proud, to believe we are better than others who don't believe our view. But Scripture changes us and makes us new creatures who are ambassadors for Christ, preaching reconciliation to God (2 Corinthians 5:17–21).

# CHAPTER 7

# WHERE ARE WE TODAY?

Refreshingly, we are seeing many lovers of their families and our country stand up to the tyrants and their tyranny. The need for God's vengeance against these forces of darkness for His elect has never been greater. As mentioned earlier in Luke 18, we have some of the strongest language used for a promise and it's made by Christ Himself, on the condition we cry out night and day unto the Father to avenge us of our enemies. If you have never prayed before and feel far from God, you must start by inviting Christ into your life. John 1:12–13 says, "But as many as received Him, to them He gave power to become the sons of God, even to them that believe on His Name: which are born, not of blood, nor of the will of the flesh, nor of the will of man, but of God."

This simple act of faith has all the power of the Creator of the universe behind it, as does His promise in Luke 18 to avenge His elect speedily.

We're at the edge of the greatest blessings ever bestowed on our planet by God—not because of our own goodness necessarily but because of His great promises to Israel that spill over to us Gentiles as promised in Romans, chapter 11.

Most Bible teachers are not Bible readers. A rather famous Bible teacher in our small town admitted he had never read the Bible from cover to cover but had listened to it once on tape while he drove back and forth to church and home. This is far more typical than you might think, but it gets worse. I asked that same teacher if he had ever considered giving His whole life to Christ? His reply: "No, because I don't want to suffer." This answers why full-life-surrender preaching never came from his mouth, and when it was square before him in Scripture he had no real comment, and his life experiences with Christ were mostly from his teen years. I've questioned many a man if he had sought victory over sin, to which they replied they did, but it did not work. Then I asked if they sought God with their whole heart, and their heads dropped in shame. "And ye shall seek Me, and find Me, when you shall search for Me with all your heart" (Jeremiah 29:13).

Another prominent pastor in our small town was arguing about an interpretation of the first two chapters of the Bible concerning creation. Finally I said, "Why can't you just believe what it says?" His reply was shocking: "Anything but that." Wow, that's unbelief on steroids! My purpose here is to jolt you loose from Bible teachers and connect you to the Author of the Bible to get you to reading and believing it for yourself. If you need more faith, ask for it from Christ the Author and finisher of our faith. Also as the man who was desperate for Christ to heal his son cried out when Jesus asked Him if he believed that He could heal his son: "I believe, Lord, but help my unbelief." And fulfill Christ's words to "call no man your teacher for one is your teacher, even Christ." Jeremiah 31:33–34 and Hebrews 11:8 declare we are taught of God Himself.

Many reading this have bravely said no to the jab, as it's referred to, but many haven't and are worried about future side effects. Israel has almost the highest jab rate amongst nations, and I keep talking about their restoration. God takes vengeance on the wicked in Jeremiah 30 at the same time that He restores Israel in chapter 31, according to the first verse in chapter 31. All of this to point out in chapter 30:12–13:

> Thus saith the LORD: Thy bruise is incur-
> able, and thy wound is grievous. There is none to

plead thy cause, that thou mayest be bound up,
thou hast no healing medicines.

I was taken to these scriptures when the reports of side effects started raging. Now, as we keep reading, Jeremiah 30:17 says:

For I will restore health unto thee, and I will
heal thee of thy wounds, saith the LORD; because
they called thee an Outcast, saying, this is Zion,
whom no man seeketh after.

Note that the Lord heals them because the whole unbelieving world and "church" is rejecting Israel (Jeremiah 30:14–16).

If we can assume we're living in the latter days, then consider the words of Jeremiah that the LORD gave him at the end of this chapter. Jeremiah 30:23–24 says:

Behold the whirlwind of the LORD goeth
forth with fury, a continuing whirlwind: it shall
fall with pain upon the head of the wicked. The
fierce anger of the LORD shall not return, until
He has performed the intents of His heart: in the
latter days ye shall consider it.

Latter day promises to fix our corrupt world. Isaiah 26:9 says, "when Thy judgements are in the earth, the inhabitants of the world will learn righteousness." The next verse really nails the corrupt elite of today: "Let favor be showed to the wicked, yet he will not learn righteousness; in the land of uprightness will he deal unjustly, and will not behold the majesty of the LORD."

In Matthew 12:17–21, we don't have a nonjudgmental, tolerant-of-evil Jesus as some would twist, but rather the powerful, confident encourager of good men and women, "till he sends forth judgement unto victory." Make no mistake: God is not glossing over the sins of mankind, especially of the USA and Israel. The scriptures in Jeremiah 30:12–17 seem to point directly to the effects of the jab, and God takes responsibility for wounding Israel and the USA because of their gross multiple sins against Him. In verse 17, God restores health and heals them, for as this healing is coupled with a born-again experience as stated in the next chapter in Jeremiah 31:31–37. Only God can do this work.

The religious teachers of our day, both in America and Israel, are in the gravest danger of severe punishment from God for their tolerance of evil and tyrants; they have turned the hearts of their congregations into fatalistic, powerless pew warmers without a hope in Christ as Lord over all, not willing that any should perish but all come to repentance. Where the Spirit of the Lord is, there is liberty, not slavery to sin and tyranny.

Zionists have wanted Israel's restoration since the late 1800s. One of the Jewish groups that has opposed them says only God can do this restoration. As it often is with factions, they both are correct. Jesus's parable of the fig tree tells of a dormant fig tree planted in the land that comes to life. We see that dormant fig tree planted in the land today, and, true to His Word, Israel has possibly the lowest percentage of Jewish Christians of any other country in the world (approximately a half of one percent). But that time is coming when ten men will take ahold of the shirt of a Jew saying, "We will go with you for we hear God is with you." Read the entire account of men seeking God in Zechariah 8:21–23.

So as we go forward, we need God's strength. We're in a dangerous position without it. Listen to Isaiah 27:5: "Or let him take hold of my strength, and he shall make peace with me." Ask God for His strength and avoid a war with Him. Our money still says, In God we trust.

# CHAPTER 8

# When the Enemy Comes in Like a Flood

So many are saying it's like we're living in a movie. And we're conditioned from thousands of movies that good prevails by killing the bad guys at the top of the evil plot to take over the world. So we're conditioned to sit back and eat popcorn until the good guys prevail. Our pulpits are to blame for such a passive response to real evil; and furthermore, the fence-sitting pulpit cowards have set back and invited more evil to enter into our country by turning a blind eye and teaching that Jesus's return at the rapture will save us from this horrific "movie." Even in Revelations the antichrist wears out the saints. The saints in the great tribulation obviously have great spiritual faith, and their prayers are heard in heaven to avenge their innocent blood, but as Scripture cannot be broken, they, not us, have to wait for Armageddon (Revelations 6:9–10).

I repeat: According to Scripture, the rapture comes at a time of peace and safety, and people know approximately when but not the day or the hour, and like the parable of the ten virgins, they drop everything to go out to meet Him. Others are so carefree that they carry on with weddings, eating, and drinking, just like before Noah's flood. Today's events don't match Scripture at all as to before the rapture. Supposed smart people point to Jesus's statement that "you will hear of wars and rumors of wars," but they don't even finish the verse that says, "see that you be not troubled: for all these things must come to pass, but the end is not yet" (Matthew 24:6).

We're bombarded today with evil of every sort globally. This is not just a local but worldwide pandemic of evil, which only the One who holds every atom together can fix. It fits perfectly to what was foretold in Scripture, even down to the jab, as to how it will be right before Israel is completely restored.

I was told to go outside and was asked, "What do you see?" It was predawn, so I said, "I see light overcoming darkness." Our whole world is very dark, but light will expose it and allow us to see clearly what God has created for man. And the darkness will drive people to the light. It's refreshing to see people on the front lines of this great battle with the forces of darkness turning to Christ for help with great faith. The ones who should be at the forefront of battle are oftentimes working directly with the enemy to get their congregations to submit to the tyrants of darkness.

Listen to the verses for which this chapter was named. Isaiah 59:19–20 says:

> So shall they fear the name of the LORD from the west, and His glory from the rising of the sun. *When the enemy shall come in like a flood* [emphasis mine], the Spirit of the LORD shall lift up a standard against him. And the Redeemer shall come to Zion, and unto them that turn from transgression in Jacob, saith the LORD.

Notice the global effects of the LORD's standard against the enemy's flood of evil: fear of the name of the LORD from the west and His glory from the east. Both east and west end up fearing God but for different reasons. Also notice it's the LORD who raises up the standard against the enemy. There's no glory of man's standard, but this standard is so holy that it must be of God and by Him. Also, note how this scripture is written especially for today's situation. It's been rightfully used throughout history, but only now do all the components of this scripture fit perfectly. The west has knowledge of Christ and has yet to actually fear even the mention of His name. The east needs to see the coming glorious miracles to fear Him. The Redeemer (Christ) coming to Zion and Romans 11:26 Deliverer coming out of Zion is paired together perfectly for Israel's salvation and restoration.

The next chapter in Isaiah jumps to the end of the great tribulation and into the thousand-year reign of Christ. We can easily tell the difference between the seven weeks of Daniel (restoration and salvation of all Israel) and the thousand-year reign by the absence of the sun for light in the thousand-year reign of Christ, because Jesus is the light in His reign. This might seem impossible for the average person, but remember Jesus holds every atom together (Colossians 1:16–17). Also, light was created on day one in Genesis 1, but the sun and the moon were created on day four.

The day of vengeance that brings Israel and America back to God will include angels and a host of other supernatural events that I've failed to mention yet. There is a strong possibility that many of the predictions of judgments in Isaiah 61–66 will be part of that, but for sure Isaiah 62:7 is our job now: "And give Him no rest, till He make Jerusalem a praise in the earth." Jesus's judgments He tells about in the parable of the tares (Matthew 13:24–51) will happen first. The righteous shining forth as the sun is the resulting blessing of these judgments. This will totally change the world. Professionals who have been hired to explain away scripture for itchy ears will be burnt most likely outside Jerusalem as in the last verses of Isaiah. Our ultimate guide should always be that nothing can contradict Scripture.

The position of believers today is clearly for all to be crying out to God for His promises to be fulfilled to avenge us of our enemies and bring about the complete restoration of Israel as He has promised. Ezekiel 36:21–28 perfectly matches Israel's spiritual state right now, God's reason for restoring Israel, and His method of doing it: Israel has profaned God's name among the heathen, so God will sanctify Israel before the eyes of the heathen, by taking out their hearts of stone and giving them hearts of flesh.

The enemy within is entrenched in positions of power worldwide and has attempted to separate us from our God by our sins. Much like Israel, we need a clean new heart and God's purge of the evil among us, and His commands need to be written in our hearts along with a Holy fear of departing from them.

# CHAPTER 9

# BLASTING THE ENEMY OUT OF OUR WORLD

Our own sins against God are oftentimes hidden from us by our spiritual blindness. Direct preaching against common sins is often avoided by listening to preachers, who refuse to even mention a common "Christian" sin but call out sins of those outside the church walls. We might at first think that we are not doing this; others, but not us. Stay with me here. I'm going to expose a short list of sins that shouldn't create any controversy, since they are very clear in the New Testament. I don't like repetitiveness, but it's necessary to group these together and expound on them even though I've mentioned some before.

*Abortion* is so prevalent in America that almost every adult has had some exposure to this monstrous evil. Almost no one is forced to have an abortion, and with crisis pregnancy centers in virtually every town, there's real help. The wholesale slaughter of the innocent has reached well above 60 million. This sin is so abhorrent that by the time Christ was born in Bethlehem, child sacrifice had been eliminated from Hebrew life; but that didn't stop Herod from murdering every child two years old and under in an attempt to eliminate King Jesus. Herod died shortly afterward.

Many people in an expectant mother's life have responsibilities to protect the unborn. First and foremost is the responsibility of the mother; second is the father; third is the parents of the mother and father; fourth is the grandparents of the expectant mother and father. Next is friends and acquaintances. If you don't step up, you'll never know the joys of watching that person grow up, only deep regrets for enabling such a murder to take place. Do what you can: something as simple as an encouraging word or offering your home to them.

Many women know the birthday that their aborted child would have been born. Decades later, every person they meet that age, they think, *That would be the age of my child.* If we even hear of a woman murdering her own children, we think of a crazy person. But that's not the worst of it. What other people think is small in comparison to God. He has said things like, "You have murdered My children." He even went so far as to say He would not forgive the sins of Manasseh because he filled Jerusalem with innocent blood.

The Hollywood elite have tried to popularize abortion, going so far as to celebrate their sin of having their own children murdered. Research Adrenochrome: who uses it and how it is made! But the bad actions of others don't excuse us. Many pastors have failed to even endorse Pro Life candidates to eliminate this great evil; their judgement is coming soon. So ask God for Him to shine His light into our hearts and reveal what needs to be confessed to Him as the horrific sin that it is. Isaiah 1 says: "Come now and let us reason together, saith the Lord: though your sins be as scarlet, they shall be white as snow; though they be red like crimson, they shall be as wool." Both scarlet and crimson are the color of blood.

*Adultery* is so common that it's simply accepted in most churches as something for which there is no cure. No human cure but Christ has been given all power in heaven and earth. Something we used to take for granted prior to the 1960s was modest dress for women. The warning that men would go to hell for even looking to lusting after women put a natural fear of God in women to not dress provocatively so as not to be a party to that lust. As my testimony highlighted the godly nature of the girls at the Christian café, their modest dress was a huge part of their godly nature. It would have been impossible to reflect such a heavenly glow without modest dress. The rage amongst churchgoing women to wear tights that reveal all their shape: it is nudity for any male with even the poorest of imaginations.

It's the task of the older women to encourage the younger women to love their husbands and children and to dress modestly (Titus 2:3–5). Men should not have to engage in this godly task with other women; it's clearly the task of women who are both older, wiser, and godly. In 1 Corinthians 7:1–5, Paul offers a cure to the lust problem of both sexes: marriage with exclusive access to each other's body. The world has distorted God's creation of male and female to signify everything but a loving couple committed solely to each other having all the intimacy each desires with each other and selflessly raising godly children. Only Christ in us can return us to God's plan for each of us. God is so set on this standard that if we don't give our bodies to our spouse, we are defrauding them. Read the scripture for yourself.

Praying for women who are not modestly dressed accomplishes two things: giving God access to change her and setting our eyes on God Himself. Another thing that helps is making a covenant with your eyes as Job did to not look upon a maid. Give them complete privacy by not looking. That whoremongers would end up in hell seems to be something apostle Paul made very clear. The man who lusts after females with pornography in the imagination is in grave danger. The no-commitment, no-children nature of this sin has wrecked many a home, and as it floods the minds of our youth. It destroys that longing for a family and replaces it with no-commitment lust. Only Christ can set the slaves to this sin free. The natural desire for long-term commitment toward your own wife and children will return with many blessings.

*Keeping a day every week set apart for God* is almost foreign to today's church, but when I was a kid, everything was closed, and a Sunday drive would necessitate filling the gas tank by Saturday night. It might help us to remember Christ's words that man wasn't built for the Sabbath but the Sabbath for man. We had a man who worked occasionally for us who would never take a Sabbath but professed faith in Christ. After decades of nonstop working, now because of chronic illness he is unable to work at all. When America observed a Sabbath, it was the nation that loaned out the most money, and even a janitor could buy a house and support his stay-at-home wife and children. Now we owe the most as a nation and personally. We still talk about the Ten Commandments but preach as if there were only nine.

*Cremation* was never once practiced in the New Testament and not until recently was it practiced in the church. "From ashes to ashes" comes out of the mouth of many a preacher/teacher, but not only does it make no sense, it is never mentioned in the Bible. When it was commanded in the Old Testament, it was done as a punishment. In Amos 2:1, a whole nation was punished for the cremation of one man.

Other gods, such as science fiction, *Harry Potter* witchcraft, and many others have to be rejected. I was talking to a young man who expressed interest in Christ one day, and he revealed he was raised a Wiccan. When my fellow evangelist came up, I asked him to talk to the boy. I stood back and observed some sort of spiritual confusion that prevented the boy from really understanding what we were talking about. It seemed to be swirling about him like electrons around the nucleus of an atom. So I simply prayed those spirits would be bound. The spirits stopped, and the boy was almost at perfect peace to listen, yet he lacked one thing. I stopped the conversation and told him he would have to renounce Wicca to receive Christ! He said he would, so he renounced Wicca on the spot and received Christ and His wonderful salvation.

No matter how harmless it may seem, it's another god. Astrology, Scientology, and any other thing that exalts itself above the knowledge of God in Christ Jesus must be renounced before you become a person whom God can bless with Himself. Don't ignore this great sin; only Christ can truly illuminate its evil and remove it further than the east is from the west.

*Lying,* of course, is extremely common, and slander is the form of lying that is mentioned in the Ten Commandments. Most are pawns in lying just by listening to professional paid liars like the mainstream media and parroting their fake news. Big government, big media, big pharmaceutical, and all their pawns have shaped every narrative of COVID-19, while many medical and other professionals would rather lose their jobs and other freedoms than take the jab. Over 12,700 doctors and scientists have signed the "Physician Declaration," which accuses COVID policy makers who have blocked early multidrug treatments of COVID-19 of crimes against humanity. Every Communist dictatorship censors the news to its citizens. Beware of becoming their slandering pawn.

Changing grace into unashamed immorality is extremely common even though it should be obvious to any true believer. Let the peace of God that passes all understanding guide you. Jude 4 exposes these corrupt teachers for what they are.

Beware of anyone wanting and accepting the praise of men. In John 5:44, Jesus said, "How can you believe which receive honor one from another and seek not the honor that cometh from God only?"

Giving should further the gospel worldwide, and every believer should have an answer for everyone for the hope that is within him. Megachurches started in the seventies ended up stopping the zeal of the Jesus Movement. The megachurch movement changed the "come to Jesus" message on every true believer's lips to "come to the concert," then "come to church." The home churches of the Jesus Movement were sadly replaced, and so was the zeal for Christ alone.

A genuine believer can slip away from a close walk with Jesus and have it replaced with a working-for-God counterfeit. No death-to-self, being-crucified-with-Christ life, but rather than hearing the voice of the Son of God as in John 10, they became carnal, and, like the Corinthians, divide up into groups and identify themselves with men or denominations instead of Christ alone. What's with so many pastors working out and then wearing tight-fitting, muscle-showing shirts to be eye candy for the women in the congregation? What's up with so many divorced men as deacons and elders? Paul's instructions on this are clear, and we need God's grace to right our wrongs.

Justice in our country has nearly vanished as our churches have not sought it diligently for the unborn. Remember, it was a church movement against slavery called abolitionism that ended slavery in America, and before that diligent Christians had ended slavery in the entire British empire. Abraham Lincoln's statement still rings true today: "Those who deny freedom to others deserve it not for themselves; and under a just God cannot long retain it."

*Fervent, effectual prayer* has almost disappeared from our churches. Peter was prayed out of prison, and Herod, who wanted Peter dead, found God's vengeance on himself a few days later and was eaten by worms. The church prayed all night until they were stopped by Peter knocking at their door. The account in Acts 12:5 simply says, "Peter therefore was kept in prison: but prayer was made without ceasing of the church unto God for him." Certainly convicting to me about the January 6 political prisoners in Washington, DC, that we need to be fervently praying for their release.

Blasting the enemy out of our world starts with ourselves. Jesus spent thirty years without much of a ministry, then He asked John the Baptist to baptize Him. His water baptism was also a baptism in the Holy Ghost with the Father announcing, "This is My beloved Son, in whom I am well pleased." Then He was tempted of the devil to depart from the will of God. Then angels came and ministered unto Him. After this, Jesus took on the world of religion and secular powers and offered spiritual freedom to everyone who believed in Him. There's no close second to Jesus Christ changing the world for good, but the ones next in line are His followers. Christ is the power source giving His followers direct access to the Father, who also gives the Holy Spirit to them who ask Him. Let us therefore fear, "lest a promise being left us of entering into His rest, any of you should seem to come short of it" (Hebrews 4:1).

One of the main purposes in writing this book is to start people praying for the day of vengeance of our God to comfort all who mourn. These words are found in Isaiah 61:2. We are familiar with the words before these because they are the words that Christ read in the synagogue and then declared: "Today this scripture is fulfilled in your ears." The scripture Jesus read is Isaiah 61:1–2:

> The Spirit of the Lord God is upon me;
> because the LORD hath anointed me to preach
> good tidings unto the meek; he hath sent me to

bind up the brokenhearted, to proclaim liberty
to the captives, and the opening of the prison to
them that are bound. To proclaim the acceptable
year of the LORD...

It continues to declare: "and the day of vengeance of our God
to comfort all who mourn." This has yet to be fulfilled, but as that
first church prayed Peter out of prison and Herod to his judgment,
so we too, as the widow in Luke 18 obtained like vengeance on her
enemies, so we too need to pray like we have never prayed before.

I repeat, the promise has not been fulfilled, and the church has
not been awakened to pray. In Jeremiah 25, this day of vengeance
sounds much like in Jeremiah 30. It's described as a whirlwind, and
it declares that the slain of the LORD shall be at that day from one end
of the earth to the other. They shall not be lamented, neither gathered nor buried; they shall be dung upon the earth. This is starting
to match the sentiment of freedom-loving people toward the tyranny
of the tyrants. The perfect thing is that vengeance is the LORD's, not
ours: but afterward, God does expect us to maintain His righteousness upon the earth.

King Solomon, in his God-given wisdom when he had finished
the temple, had a long prayer to God that was centered around man's
departure from God, God's punishment of that departure, then man's
return to God. Then he asks God to forgive Israel's sins and restore
them. Here is God's reply:

If I shut up heaven that there be no rain, or
if I command the locusts to devour the land, or
if I send pestilence among My people; if My people, which are called by My name, shall humble
themselves, and pray, and seek My face, and turn
from their wicked ways; then will I hear from
heaven, and will forgive their sin, and will heal
their land. (2 Chronicles 7:13–14)

God goes on to warn Solomon of departing from God, and promises complete exile from the land if he served other gods. As history unfolded, Solomon did depart from God, and eventually the entire nation was split in two, then one at a time sent into exile. The part of Israel that had the tribe of Judah was eventually taken captive for seventy years in Babylon before they were restored back to the land and Jerusalem restored. Then later, as Christ promised, they would be killed and led away captive into all nations, and Jerusalem will be trodden down by the Gentiles until the times of the Gentiles be fulfilled (Luke 21:24). Jerusalem will be totally restored with the completion of the Temple as promised in Ezekiel 40–44. Ezekiel 45 sets apart Jerusalem for only the tribes of Jerusalem. In Ezekiel 46, a stream comes from the altar, flows to the Dead Sea, and heals the Dead Sea. Then Israel expands its borders without war.

AD 70 fulfilled the part of being taken captive to all nations. Then Israel becoming a nation again in 1948, or 1,888 years later, started the second part, as we see Jerusalem still trodden down by Gentiles even though Jerusalem was taken in 1967. Israel is still that dormant fig tree planted in the land awaiting its new birth (leaves on the fig tree). Judgments of God happen as promised but can easily be avoided by seeking God's face and repenting of our wicked ways. Jesus stated that no man has seen God at any time, but the Son has revealed Him (John 1:18). Seek Jesus, find the Father.

Worship is heavily emphasized today, but not godly living by the power of God. Jesus stated, "You worship Me in vain because you teach for doctrine the traditions of men."

It's hard to write this short book without an altar call to every reader. To be loved by the One who created the universe is no small thing, but our sins have separated us from Him, and nobody but we can confess and repent of our sins. The corporate sins of our nation feel like it's someone else's duty, but, remember, we are the United States of America that proudly professes trust in God on every piece of money. Instead of dividing ourselves through departure from God, we need to be praying and encouraging every soul to return to God so He can heal us and then our land.

Some of the hardest cases of individuals make the best converts because they can now see both sides. Take Mike Lindell, for instance, the "My Pillow" guy. He was saved out of drug addiction and is now evangelizing and leading the charge to the Supreme Court to fix the 2020 elections. I was also a hard case.

Before turning to the next chapter, take some time to invite Christ into your life to shine His light inside you and help you turn from every sin that He shows you. Call on Him to save you to the uttermost and separate you from your sins further than the east is from the west.

# CHAPTER 10

# WINNING

One thing that is helpful to see is how people do things that seem so contrary to their own best interests, especially conservatives in office. The vast network of evil can entrap and blackmail people or threaten or bribe them, but the best trick of all is to make them believe a lie. No other method gives such convincing results as the creation of an innocent human believing a lie. Our divisions in America are mostly products of deception. The good news is this form of manipulation is easily destroyed by God's vengeance and supernatural revelations. Sweeping changes will happen as righteous free people get their country back and demand the end of electronic voting and tabulation, ballot harvesting, mail-in ballots, and dirty voter rolls.

The above paragraph might seem misplaced, but it might help our prayers to be more focused on the massive undertaking this is, and to keep our focus on Christ to destroy the enemy. Compromise is what got us here. Purity in mind and actions is the step it takes to win in the war room.

A few years back, Sherwood Pictures released a movie called *War Room*. It was a powerful film and is highly recommended to improve our prayer life. It shot unexpectedly to number one and changed so many lives. Teens were telling me they had seen it twice, because it reminded them of their mom or grandmother. The movie used very ordinary people to get an extraordinary principle across to the masses. I hope you buy a copy; it's great to see and to loan out.

I'm not a person who fights for lost causes neither do I encourages others to do so. Winning in this case is as a *united* team that bravely endures critics, death threats, slander, and distractions, then perseveres in prayer and anything God calls us to.

Thinking back on the dozens of answered prayers that were huge (even effecting the life and death of five of our family members), there is one thing all those prayers had in common: fervency. What do I mean by fervent praying? I mean passionate, sincere requests that cannot be ignored. Few people pray like that, mostly because they have no idea that God can hear them, for they haven't done what I address in the previous chapter. Real, sincere Christians can boldly approach the throne of grace (undeserved divine assistance). Remember: "He that spared not His own Son, but delivered Him up for us all, how shall He not with Him also freely give us all things" (Romans 8:32).

Probably the time of my most intense prayer took place in a snowstorm. It had been a warm sunny autumn day, and my son-in-law, three grandchildren, our youngest daughter, and six of their friends where hiking to the top of Tehachapi peak. The weather quickly changed, and they were lost in a whiteout snowstorm. They had called us for help. They asked for our son, Mark, specifically since he knew that mountain like nobody else. They also asked for Mark to use the Find My Friends app to give them both a direction to head toward.

There were already several inches of snow at the trail head when we all arrived. Mark had taken great care to dress properly and had lots of flashlights and as much warm clothing as his pack would hold. Mark took off at a brisk pace, knowing he didn't have much daylight left and how complete darkness could really mess things up. I started praying fervently for the snow to stop. I had a few months of asking off and on to be crucified with Christ as Paul was in Galatians 2:20. So I promised God I would pray every day to be crucified with Christ. The snow instantly went from large one-and-a-half-inch flakes to cornflake-size, then like glitter, then to nothing within seconds. I was overjoyed, and I was given real peace that everyone would be all right.

A few minutes later, I got a call from Mark that he had found three of them because they were yelling back to the other eight, and he was now heading toward the eight. Ten minutes later, I got another call that he had found them all and was passing out flashlights. Just as he said that, the last bit of light was gone. We sent a couple of men to follow Mark's footprints in the snow with arms full of jackets and blankets. The eleven kept coming along the trail, some with ice in their hair and all very tired and hungry. I think almost every one of them asked me if the promised prime-rib dinner was still going to happen. We put them in vehicles that had been left on with the heaters on high and started off the mountain. When everyone was safe and off the mountain, the blizzard resumed worse than ever. At dinner, Spenser told us how she had prayed fervently for the wind to stop twice, and it did both times. I told them my story. God and Mark were held in the highest regard, and I can't ever remember such grateful praying at a dinner table.

I noticed a couple of young tree squirrels playing outside a few minutes ago and enjoyed watching them chase each other up and down and around a tree. It was probably a busy year for them gathering so many acorns free for the taking. The deer have gotten huge this year with the abundance of acorns. Probably the largest three-pointer I've ever seen was lying on the front lawn this morning. This carefree lifestyle of the animal kingdom is supposed to teach us something. Jesus said, "Behold the birds of the air. They don't sow or reap or gather into barns, yet your heavenly Father feeds them. Are ye not much better than they?"

Freedom is something we take for granted, but our forefathers who shaped our government with the help of God the Father surely didn't take freedom for granted. They were sick of tyrannical kings and church combinations dictating to them and robbing them of their God-given freedom to create wealth and have real liberty and justice for all. A mid-18th century revival had put liberty and justice for all in the heart of most Americans, but a constitutional government with checks and balances based on the Bible had never been tried. It was conceived in the Magna Carta in England but lacked the force to free them from the king and church combination. "Where the Spirit of the Lord is there is liberty" is written in the Bible, but after the revival it was written in their hearts. So powerful was this freedom through Christ that the battle cry of the revolution was "No king but King Jesus."

A vigorous attempt to abolish slavery was made both at the Declaration of Independence and the Constitutional Convention. Both times, the Southern states threatened to side with Britain against us. It wasn't until another revival in the 1830s that the thought of actually having freedom and justice for all Americans began to take a strong roots again. The catalyst was the success of the devout Christians in England led by William Wilberforce, who abolished slavery in the entire British Empire. This, in turn removed the South's move to side with our enemy Britain. This put considerable pressure to eliminate that evil practice.

New states were coming into the union, and there was great debate on whether they should be free or slave. Most people detested slavery in the western expansion, and states were typically free. The accumulation of power by starting a political party by the antislavery group and actually getting Abraham Lincoln on the ballot as the first Republican presidential candidate infuriated the Democrats. When he won the election, they started seceding from the Union. The desperation of these powerful men was on full display to continue slavery.

The war was bloody as the resolve of each side strengthened. The North was singing "The Battle Hymn of the Republic," which contained the line "As He died to make men holy, let us die to make men free." Abraham Lincoln was rapidly growing in character. Lincoln said things like, "Many say God is on their side, but what matters is: are we on God's side?" Abraham Lincoln wasn't a Christian until the train ride to Gettysburg in late 1863. He finally surrendered to Christ in spite of all the hypocrisy he had seen. The President revised his original address after encountering the unfathomable Christ, and wrote a speech that only lasted a couple of minutes. Today that speech is etched in stone in the Lincoln Memorial.

Civil war was a painful and incomplete solution to what was going on in the South. Lincoln recognized the need to rebuild the South without slavery at its core. The Emancipation of the Southern slaves was an act of spoils of war and if the purpose of the war was to be permanent, Lincoln needed a constitutional amendment to outlaw slavery, because to end the war without it would allow the South to resume business as usual. The Democrats wanted to switch parties to vote for the amendment, but Lincoln wanted it passed into law by both Democrats and Republicans. Lincoln wanted unity, and the union side couldn't live up to its name without it. The amendment was passed and the war ended; less than a week later, Lincoln was assassinated. All the plans to heal the wounds of that bloody war died with Lincoln, and revenge and punishment of the South took its place.

Finney, the firebrand of the preceding revival, was very much against the idea of civil war, but he seemed to offer no other solutions. Today, a fire is brewing toward civil war in the minds of many. It seems unavoidable to many in our pulpits. Our minds and hearts need to be gathered to God Himself if we are going to avoid this catastrophe. We need to turn to what Abraham Lincoln saw after meeting the True Founder of our country on that somber train ride to Gettysburg.

> Four score and seven years ago, our fathers brought forth on this continent, a new nation, conceived in Liberty, and dedicated to the proposition that all men are created equal... [T]hat these dead shall not have died in vain—that this nation, under God, shall have a new birth of freedom—and that government of the people, by the people, for the people, shall not perish from the earth.

As the scriptures declares: "Where the Spirit of the LORD is there is Liberty." We have no options to true liberty. The "liberty" the left is selling is slavery to sin. The liberty of God is: "If the Son shall set you free, you shall be free indeed" (John 8). Our religion is tainted with self-righteousness and self-interest, big ministries where their followers talk of their leaders and heap praises on them. No such religion exists in God's kingdom.

Winning is building a nation of prayer warriors who will not stop praying until they have God's ear; who will stop at nothing in their abandonment and devotion to God to get it, seeking God with our whole hearts and surrendering all of what we own and are to Him. Our prayers can be general or specific but always must be directed to our Father in heaven in the name of His Son Jesus Christ of Nazareth. David's prayer was full of emotion, pleading, and urgency. David's faith was expanded by the author and finisher of his faith as he fervently went directly to God with his pleadings and often asked to be avenged of his enemies, just as we should be doing at this time in history.

# CHAPTER 11

# THE GREATEST REVIVAL OF ALL TIME

The greatest revival of all time is started by God, continued by God, powered by God, and believed by His saints. The apostle Paul saw this coming revival as he reasoned with converted Jews and Gentiles who had given up on the possibility of the kingdom returning to Israel and all Israel being saved as Scripture says. Listen to Paul's words as he sees what only God can do:

> Now if the fall of them be the riches of the world, and the diminishing of them be the riches of the Gentiles; how much more their fullness? …For if the casting away of them be the reconciling of the world, what shall the receiving of them be, but life from the dead? (Romans 11:12–15)

Ezekiel 37 is one of the largest life-from-the-dead events of the greatest revival: with a great army risen up from the dead; that is, all the tribes of Israel, also God will open the graves worldwide of all the tribes of Israel. Many Old Testament saints such as David as king, and shepherd, Elijah as one that turns the hearts of the fathers, to the children and hearts of the children to the fathers (Malachi 4). In addition the deliverer comes out of Zion to turn ungodlyness away from Jacob (Romans 11). The judgment on the wicked and healing from the jab in Jeremiah 30, and the complete restoration of Israel in chapter 31 bring many gentiles to Christ and to Jerusalem with a Jew among them.

That glorious insight into America having a new birth of freedom by Abraham Lincoln will come to fruition, not solely due to the efforts of man but the power of God finally depended on by His people. Corruptible people saying no to sin by the power of God: a clarity of belief, hearing the voice of the Son of God and watching Him and His saints claim the prayer of "Thy will be done on earth as in heaven," and the command to "go make disciples of all nations."

Watching the Lord regenerate, restore, and rebuild Jerusalem and all Israel is full of supernatural miracles, thus no nation will be able to deny that God is real and that His Word is true. Massive evangelism will circle the globe, and the gospel will be published in every nation as Christ said in Matthew 13:10. Note there are fifty-seven countries where the Bible is outlawed, so there are massive changes coming.

"Choose you this day whom you will serve" is a theme of Scriptures, and every great revival has a call to choose God by repentance of our sins. The gospel means "good news." It's not good news to lift up eternal godly standards with no power to fulfill them. There was no lack of God's laws being taught when Christ Jesus walked the earth, but the power from God Himself to aid us was the missing ingredient that Christ proclaimed. That was truly good news. Real forgiveness, along with regeneration of the believer, was all made possible because Christ went to the cross and died in our place for our sins.

This greatest revival hits at the heart of the problem of the masses' "willful ignorance." Critical race theory doesn't have a chance in an intelligent person but flourishes in the willfully ignorant. The intelligent person must examine the opposition's arguments and weigh the validity or falsity of each side; if more independent study is needed, he must find sources that are accurate in displaying all the facts. It's impossible to keep God's view out of almost any subject; that's why the Bible was the most quoted resource of our Founding Fathers. Men who don't know the Bible are vulnerable to brainwashing, and we could even say that many are willfully ignorant. How can the best-selling book every year (I believe) since the invention of the printing press be ignored?

Selfishness is what the great reset is trying to exploit, while the great revival will destroy selfishness and transform many of the willfully ignorant into intelligent people who love God. Primarily the willfully ignorant suffer from brainwashing that was developed to control people, and separation from such tactics takes God's intervention to regenerate one's whole being from darkness to light. People will go along with a group to feel secure, which is wonderful if it's a group of people who have been connected to Christ by Christ alone. But worldly or theological group affiliations tend to lead them back to ignorance. Small differences and lively discussion are beneficial to intelligent people, but are avoided by the willfully ignorant because they can't deal with facts and reason. This is where we get the term "unreasonable people," due to their obvious inability to reason things through. We usually give up and write them off as a lost cause.

Saul of Tarsus, by his own admission, was ignorant. He persecuted Christians, threw them in jail, and even forced some to blaspheme Christ. He changed in one supernatural moment when he personally met Christ as he was on his way to arrest more Christians. If those persecuted Christians were praying for their persecutor as Christ had taught, they prayed the greatest influencer ever into being: the apostle Paul. What we can't achieve ourselves, our prayers can. Nothing is too hard for God. Ask and you shall receive.

The greatest revival of all time will have David as the example to the nations and church where he has been in heaven since Jesus led captivity captive, so many nations will follow David's lead and revise their governments into godly, biblical governments that will result in vast godliness and prosperity for many nations. "One nation under God" will become common. The gospel that doesn't change nations will be scorned by many.

The greatest revival of all time is at our very doorstep. We can play a vital part by praying for that day of vengeance to comfort all who mourn and cry day and night unto Our Father to avenge us of our enemies. Just as God delivered the children of Israel out of slavery in Egypt when He heard their crying unto Him, so will He deliver us from the rising dictators of our day.

Revival in the persecuted underground church in China has been ongoing since the mideighties. Their hunger has always been for the Bible, to read it and to have their own copy. Many successful efforts are trying to fill this need. Dictators have always banned the Bible when they got the power to do so. The greatest fear of dictators is intelligent Bible-believers. So great is that fear of the coming dictators plan to reduce the population of earth to 500 million people. Over 90 percent will be murdered if they are successful. I don't believe they will be; and furthermore, I believe it will be the end of them. It only makes sense that these powerful people hated the most nationalist president in decades and were desperate to destroy him. Remember Jesus judges nations Mt. 25:31–46.

The greatest revival will last for forty-nine years, as the construction of the temple and the stream out of the altar will heal the Dead Sea, and multitudes will flock to the temple to fulfill Jesus's words that it would be a house of prayer for all people. Much of the newly acquired land will be given to strangers (Ezekiel 47:22–23) to be close as possible to God's chosen land and people. I imagine that the Lord will be constantly sending workers into the harvest to keep the revival and God's will on earth to all nations going until the Holy Spirit is taken out at the rapture and the evil one takes over, (Second Thessalonians 2:7–9). With one-sixth of the invading armies returning to their nations after the invasion of Israel, and I hope we can give each soldier a copy of the Bible in their language with Ezekiel 38–39 highlighted and a message printed to bring him to Christ and propel him into the scriptures.

It's interesting that Ezekiel 35 seems to foretell the end of Islam's hatred for America and Israel. This is located between chapter 34, where God destroys the shepherds of Israel and replaces them with David, and chapter 36, where God restores Israel. The humongous change in our world without globalist, radical Islam, false teachers, and willful ignorance running rampant: you might say it's the will of God being done on earth as it is in heaven. It will be a time of peace and safety, just as 1 Thessalonians predicts before the rapture. Another event in Luke 21:25–26 will also precede the rapture.

# CHAPTER 12

# THE GREAT REDO

What I'm calling the great redo here is the seven weeks of Daniel mentioned earlier. These seven weeks, or 49 years, will transform the entire world. You may be asking why you haven't heard about this from anywhere else. That's a great question and I believe part of the answer lies in God's desire to separate us from our Bible teachers and reconnect us to our Bibles as the only authority in our lives. The severity of judgment on the Shepherds and the principle of the flock, with David replacing the Shepherds along with the government and Israel coming to Christ (as promised but ignored by our churches) will be similar to how the resurrection of Christ was such a surprise that it totally revised how people related to God. God became close and available to all and scriptures became clear and accessible to everyone. The severity of the judgments that usher in this seven weeks of Daniel will give a clear condemnation to the clergy and rabbis of our Day. This separation from professionals and attachment to our Bibles and it's Author will be a glorious transformation of the minds and hearts of nations, but especially of America and mostly of Israel! Sometimes it takes a jolt to dislodge us from our old thinking and attach us to God Himself in His Word. As the first century disciples took the Gospel around the world the transformation was so stark that all other forms of spiritual practice were forsaken and even burned in bonfires. Jesus's half brother Jude was given the honored position of being the last letter before the book of Revelations. Jude exposes errors within the last days church but gives great hope for a correction of those errors by stating that the Lord would come with 10,000 of saints with judgments and convincing the ungodly of their errors. It would seem that this is as Jesus promises to His disciples to never forsake them and to be with them always, as reality but not visible I would assume. 10,000 divided population wise would give America about 500 saints, but probably higher communication areas might need less saints. Whatever the Lord directs will be exciting and life changing for our world; turning hard hearts into lovers of God is the greatest miracle on earth to me.

The parable of the fig tree illustration provides a perfect picture of Israel without any visible life connection to God yet all the necessary elements to come to life are there just waiting for God's command to restore them as at the first. This great harvest of souls will begin with the Son of Man sending forth His angels to remove the fake Christians from His Kingdom (tares) and burn them most likely near the entrance to Jerusalem, as in Isaiah's last verses. This dramatic judgment of false churchianity with angels probably visible for all to see and the severity of the judgements on all things that offend, will culminate in the righteous shining forth as the sun in the kingdom of their Father. (Matthew 13:37–43) This shining as the sun alone of the righteous will bring forth God's righteousness for all to see and underscore necessity of the previous judgments. The next two parables explain how to become one of these righteous. Matthew (13:44–46) This all or nothing approach to Christianity is all consuming, not just something you add to your life; rather it signifies the One that created you living inside you as Lord of everything. The amazing freedom that follows such conversions always astonishes it's captives (2 Corinthians 3:17). That fiery judgment on the perverters of the Bible will pave the way for intense study and commitment of untold millions as the parables of the mustard seed and leaven will come alive. Hint: birds and leaven are evil.

Later in Matthew 24:31 another sending forth of angels culminates in the great tribulation, but this time they only gather the elect and they are accompanied by Christ Himself and the sun is darkened.

It's important to note that some of these may be converts that Jesus had told seven years prior to "depart from me ye workers of iniquity I never knew you". The foolishness of professing believers seems to flourish as those seven weeks of Daniel come to a glorious end with the return of the Messiah. Many will miss the rapture, but hopefully they overcome the antichrist in the great tribulation and receive the glorious promised reward of ruling and reigning with Christ for a 1,000 years. These saints will be beheaded for their testimony.

Representative forms of government will vanish in Israel as David takes the throne and takes control of the spiritual leadership as well he will point the people to God to be born again as is promised over and over in their Old Testaments. America might have similar sentiments after our current experience of the takeover by the deep state. The release of the "Twitter Files" and exposure of the great reset has shaken our trust in a complicated system of alleged checks and balances. Sadly the system has consumed itself with innumerable laws and regulations that have transferred power to multiple agencies that are arguably in charge of our elected representatives, and not the other way around. It's quite refreshing to see 20 conservative Republicans hold Kevin McCarthy hostage until he agrees to their demands. On the 15th vote days later the entire world sees what firmly planted righteous people can do! The freedom caucus is small but it has put itself in charge, so we must pray fervently for God's protection and success.

Power corrupts and absolute power corrupts absolutely: this always seems to manifest itself whenever power is given to man. We could say it's the natural state of the natural man. This huge takeover by God Himself solves this problem. When Nebuchadnezzar ruled the world he was lifted up in pride but God humbled him and showed Him that God Governs in the affairs of men. Much like this prideful king who had to spend seven years eating grass like an ox and living outdoors to get the principle that God is in charge firmly planted in his being, so we will see leaders worldwide either judged or changed or both. The vast changes in the hearts of men will result in an enormous change in the governing of men; in fact, the change will be so vast that men will no longer need to be governed by the laws of men.

Instead a general sense of being governed by God Himself and HIS RIGHTEOUSNESS will so prevail over humanity that other forms of governance will only be necessary for the remaining rebels of society.

Israelites who are dead will be made alive not only at the valley of the dry bones (Ezekiel 37) but world wide (Ezekiel 37:12–14) will totally alter how people think about their lives as they hear stories of masses of people back from the Grave. Perhaps most interesting among them will be the Holocaust victims, and this will give Germany a chance to make full restitution to these victims of real hatred. Moreover, their renewed lives by God's Holy Spirit will be extremely convicting to the nation of Israel and Jews worldwide, that God's punishments are a response to our departure from Him. These great moments of repentance will spill over to the Gentile world, too, and we will see ourselves in Israel and be given a chance to repent of our blindness toward God's punishments. It's important to note that this raising of the dead is NOT like at the rapture, where we will be raised incorruptible with youthful bodies that never die, but rather as Lazarus who died again.

David's great redo is to pass the throne successfully to his descendants and unite Israel; to build the temple and receive all the promised land, putting away of all of Israel's sins and watching the nation welcome Gentiles in real faith as they flock to Jerusalem to pray at the New Temple. And, as they bring back Jews with them, this will go a long way toward healing old wounds throughout the world as humans unite around their Creator. David seems to be the king while the temple is built. The great earthquake before the massive invasion of nations against Israel levels Jerusalem but seems to leave David's fortress intact (Jeremiah 30:18). The invasion seems to occur quickly after David takes the throne, and, evidently, David stops the temptation for the Israelites to defend themselves; rather they trust totally in the scriptures that God Himself will fight for them and only 1/6$^{th}$ of their enemies survive. This great redo in faith in God alone and His scriptures (Ezekiel 38–39) also gives Israel confidence that God will do what He promises, because the powers that threaten them are so vast it takes 7 months and all Israel to bury the dead. The smell is horrible and hopefully, each grave is clearly marked for all to visit and reflect on the price paid for their hatred of God and His chosen people, in His written Word. Hopefully, the surviving 1/6th will return to their country with a Bible in their own language and start a revival. Note that burial even of God's enemies takes place, not any of the popular cremations that plague our Christian in name only churches of today. We need deep repentance of such obvious departure from God's written Word; Amos 2:1 puts an entire nation in judgment over the cremation of one man.

Let's briefly revisit the current unbelief in these end times events. The greatest event ever to effect humanity was the death, burial, and resurrection of Christ. It had no human believers before it happened, even though Christ kept restating it and scriptures like Isaiah 53 abound in scripture. Why this massive unbelief in such a vital act in the reconciliation of all mankind? The answer is twofold: First, the religious establishment seemed not only to be ignorant of Christ's death and resurrection but hostile to Christ Himself, especially since He calls them out as vile sinners in several major areas. Second, the masses constantly followed Christ around and listened to Him, yet they were not able to understand that Christ would die and resurrect from the dead. I believe the answer to this question is why we have such a hard time in our day believing all theses miracles involving Israel will take place. The teachers had conditioned Israel to look ahead to the great restoration of Israel, and, thus, skip over the suffering Christ! This hope is more alive than ever after the resurrection, just before Christ ascends into heaven with the disciples last question: "LORD, will you at this time restore again the kingdom to Israel?" Simular it is in our day that our teachers implore us to look for the rapture, the one world government, or the great tribulation; in doing so, they ignore the entire restoration of Israel, as that final question that those hopeful apostles asks Jesus finally approaches us in these Latter Days.

Perhaps the most vital redo will be in families, as during the aforementioned judgements Elijah is sent to restore all things and especially relationships in families, turning the hearts of the fathers to the children and the hearts of the children to the fathers. The next phrase is like a spiritual punch in the gut exhausting all our pride and grudges: "lest I come and smite the earth with a curse." This is the last phrase of our Old Testament and is intended to warn us to take heed to Elijah and do exactly as he says. Relationships are extremely important and the one between parents and children even has a commandment of promise that things will go well with us if we honor our parents. This great redo of our family relationships seems to focus on fathers and children; perhaps this connection is the great missing link that currently plagues our children and is responsible for their inability to function normally as husbands and wives producing godly children. Our fractured children, without belief in the eternal Creator God and His absolute standards for humanity, will be changed with Elijah's preaching uniting families as never before. The enemy of our soul has gone to great lengths to divide us with satanic hatred for what is from God thus creating what we see today. But all this evil will be vastly diminished with the most powerful preaching of all time, aided by the presence of the Holy Ghost in none other than Elijah himself, and manifesting Elijah's words to all listeners.

Our faith will grow rapidly, yet we must not allow ourselves to become spiritually lazy but must take seriously our Lord's admonition to give ourselves and our possessions to Him— to deny ourselves and pick up our cross (die to self) and follow Him. Opportunities for Evangelism will abound and we must seize them. America will be full of people ready to return to their homelands to spread the gospel, and we must send them. These new evangelists will be revered in their homelands, and open the ears and hearts of nations from a bottom up and top down approach of Evangelism. Primarily due to judgments and secondarily due to miracles with undeniable alignment to scripture, leaders will fear and revere God and His Word. Relationships with godly nations will facilitate much change. Government that is not a terror to evil (as stated in Romans 13) will be disregarded by godly nations and practices such as abortion, child and slave labor and sexual trafficking will be met with a clamor for a godly leader that rises to the throne of God. Christians everywhere will have a great redo of their faith in God's power to avenge them of their enemies and give them godly leaders. This top down, bottom up, revival will be glorious for all who love God, but His enemies will be looking for someone to take on the King of kings at the end of the great tribulation. Most will be keenly aware of scripture and the (approximate) time of the rapture as the seven weeks of Daniel approaches it's end from God's command to restore and rebuild Jerusalem, which sets the clock for the rapture, the great tribulation,and the return of the King of kings at the battle of Armageddon. This basic understanding of coming events will give the Churches a great redo in their response to the close coming of the rapture, and the peace and safety of 1 Thessalonians will be real, and, for many it will be a surprise but others will go out to meet Him, as in the parable of the 10 virgins but five will be foolish and having no experience of being tried in the fire of tribulation and having their robes made white by the blood of the Lamb (Revelation 3:18). These foolish virgins are able to talk to Jesus much like in Matt 7:22–23, where Christ says He never knew them. The verse before this discourse makes it all too clear that only those who do the will of the Father will enter the Kingdom. The verse after the discourse explains the specifics of the will of the Father as the Words that Christ has just said in the Sermon on the Mount. The solution to this faux Christianity is found in Revelations 3:20–22.

Finally, we see God's day of vengeance to comfort all who mourn, as Isaiah 61:2 comes to life; yet what happens to those who aren't mourning for all the evil on the earth we see today? This day of vengeance cast so much light and judgment upon the wicked that many of them will have a great redo from their wicked indoctrination against God and His Righteousness. Families have been divided by the current psychological doctrines that attack all that is godly. From woke news media to woke colleges a wave of darkness has enveloped the minds and hearts of so many, transforming them into soldiers of darkness for the enemy of their own souls. At last the promise of Isaiah that when thy judgments are in the earth the inhabitants thereof will learn righteousness. The lost causes that people had given up on, will come to God for a great redo of their thinking and prayers of family and friends will be miraculously answered for a redo in relationship with God first and others to follow. Education will take on a dimension of truth that, hopefully, will be so profound that people with college degrees will demand to be properly educated or their money returned to them. This will be the greatest opportunity for the righteous to shine forth as the sun. It is important to note that God never hides the sins of His servants, but uses them to teach us what to guard against, especially as the transformation of education into indoctrination almost lost the free world. The fear of the Lord as the beginning of wisdom must be front and center of any real education.

The return of David will have great compassion without compromising any of Christ's teachings, and give great sinners great hope of forgiveness and complete renewal from God Himself.

The promises in Jeremiah 30 that God will heal from the side effects of the vaccine are so vast and kind that God's true compassion will flow forth for the greatest of redos for those poor sick people with the fear of death looming over them. The medical profession and medicine will undergo a great overhaul for the good of the masses and tyrannical leaders trying to murder their own citizens will be judged severely by God's vengeance. Jeremiah 30:23–24 seems to be the greatest redo of the secular world with a judgment that doesn't end until God has accomplished His purposes. It can't be stated too often that we are required to pray to be avenged of our enemies day and night as in Luke 18:1–8.

Communists within free countries are clamoring to support the overthrow of Brazil just as they did Venezuela years before and Cuba decades before that. The banner from the protesters was: "give us the source codes". Voting machines without their source codes are a blatant admission of fraud. If there is nothing to hide then reveal the source codes! Many people worldwide are resisting the great reset and communist regimes with every ounce of their strength and, hopefully, faith in the One who has been given all power in Heaven and on earth will spring forth in them to bring lasting comfort to all who mourn.

There are great possibilities for opportunities for good from entertainment, news, and influence types of media. Renewed people must demand and participate in the redo of these industries and accept no compromise with any evil form of productions. The concept of controlling people by programming them must be abolished and Christ's presence must be everywhere with the freedom The Spirit of God alone can give.

A financial redo will recreate financial freedom for the individual. Socialism, communism, and corporate monopolies will be exposed for what they are; the individual and small business, along with private property ownership and near zero interest rates will prevail, while governments, needs are amply met without taxation as they seek lasting prosperity for all. Equity based currencies will bring an end to the legalized theft that has plagued honest hard working people for centuries.

Science could become truthful and helpful again, as fear and knowledge of God fills the mind of people with even avenge intelligence. Solutions to pollution and energy alone would bring about a great redo in the lives of every freedom loving family. Incorporating God's laws, such as a sabbath, and letting the land rest every seven years, and other principles in scripture will add the missing element whose absence has plagued our earth with pestilence and diseases.

# ADDENDUM

It's important for those with a keen interest and belief in the Bible to have more than a brief summary of biblical events; they also need a good, approximate chronology of soon-to-be-fulfilled scriptures. A good biblical foundation against popular end-times teachings will also be necessary, for these popular teachers obliterate what the Scriptures actually say, and, sadly, don't build people up into saints with victory over their own flesh by the power of God.

Always keep in mind Paul's admonishment to his churches: "Knowledge puffeth up, but love edifyeth." Our minds constantly want to be superior to others, but Paul also told us to think of others better than yourself. This is an impossible task without the power of Christ to save us to the uttermost. One thing that should be at the forefront of our conversations (as it was Paul's) is "knowing the terror of the Lord, we persuade men." Remember that God's truth is precious pearls, and we need to ask for wisdom so as not to cast them before swine, as our Lord admonished us. Sometimes the most powerful thing we can do is wipe the dust off our feet and leave. I did just that one evening in the Army when a man started mocking us. The next day, he apologized and noted our real relationship with Christ.

Love has been rebranded as tolerance of sin and false teachings: neither was tolerated by our Lord. Love cannot exist without fervently praying for the people we converse with. A Christless doctrine that seems correct may be just a better counterfeit than an obvious false doctrine. Praying without ceasing can become a way of life for those filled with the love of God, and asking and receiving as our Lord promises as we abide in Him.

Our objective cannot be to get followers of ourselves but nothing less than followers of Christ Jesus Himself. You can tell a false revival by what its followers talk about. Does it exalt Christ and His Word and a personal walk with Him, or their pastors/teachers or church?

We can ask if we are in a time of peace and safety now, and nobody would say yes to that, so the laws of logic would now demand that the rapture of the church is not near without some huge change, and that change is the greatest revival of all time. Preceding that revival are two distinct major events. First is the watchman on the wall, as in Ezekiel 33, the deliverer coming out of Zion turning ungodliness away from Jacob. Romans 11:26, and the last few verses of the Old Testament; Elijah the prophet before that coming great and dreadful day of the Lord, turning the hearts of children and fathers to each other. Then the fulfillment of judgment must begin at the household of God, and Jeremiah 25 and Ezekiel 34's judgment of the shepherds.* Next the judgment of the tares and the exalting of the righteous. In Matthew 13:37–43, Jesus is sending forth His angels for a complete cleansing of His kingdom, and then the righteous will shine as the sun. This would appear to fit together with Jude 14–15 as Christ is with every one of His ten thousand saints. Then as in Ezekiel 34, David appears on the scene, and probably also appearing are children whom King Herod murdered in an attempt to kill Christ, with those children coming from Bethlehem to their own border (Jeremiah 31:16–17). The promises of the day of vengeance in Malachi 4:5, Isaiah 61:2, and Jeremiah 30:23–24 are tied together with the judgment of the shepherds and the principle of the flock, along with the beginning of the physical and spiritual restoration of Israel.

The judgment of the rest of the world is maybe not unto death, but it falls with pain on the heads of the wicked, and it does not stop until God has accomplished the intent of His heart: in the latter days you shall consider it, and it's termed as the fierce anger of the Lord, as the scripture declares in Jeremiah 30:23–24. Ezekiel's valley of dry bones in Ezekiel 37 is probability next, producing all the tribes of Israel that have been slain from long-ago battles. This miracle seems to promote David to king over Israel, with plans to build Ezekiel's temple, probably right where the Dome of the Rock Muslim temple is. Obviously, this infuriates Muslims.

Ezekiel 38 and 39 is a spectacular battle seemingly without any Israeli involvement, but it would fit that this war is the time of Jacob's trouble that he is delivered from that massive invasion (Jeremiah 30). This war seems to be the destruction of the Muslim enemies of Israel and America that Ezekiel 35 foretells. Israel spends seven months burying the dead whom God destroys with overflowing rain, hailstones, blood, pestilence, fire, and brimstone. There's no mistake that God destroyed Israel's enemies, and Israel still apparently takes great care of them for seven months, probably marking each grave so relatives can visit. The real highlight of the war is their coming to Christ and coming totally clean of all their rebellion against God, along with His loving rebuke of them for the past couple of thousand years.

Zechariah 12:9–14 gives the details of their repentance. Much like my own testimony, they see their Messiah whom they crucified and rejected for almost two thousand years. They repent as family units, probably because they rejected individual family members who had received Christ by shunning them as a whole family. The dear Jewish brother I went to Israel with is still rejected by his family after over fifty years.

The other huge miracle is in the last part of Ezekiel 39:23–27 and Zechariah 2:11–12, when Gentiles help bring all the Jews back to Israel, and God is sanctified in the sight of many nations. This is a hypersupernatural event where God even opens the graves of Israelis worldwide and returns them to Israel (Ezekiel 36:24, 37:12). Then enemies of Israel will be gone, and the Zechariah 8:23 prophecy of ten men taking one Jew back to Israel will fill Israel.

The great earthquake in Ezekiel 38 provides the building space for the Ezekiel 40 temple to be constructed (about a quarter of the old city), and probably much gold and silver from all over the world from the arrival of David helps facilitate building this magnificent temple. The Ezekiel 38 war was seemingly partly fueled by the desire to seize these treasures. The pinnacle of the temple is that after its completion, the stream of water that flows out from underneath the altar turns into a river that flows east to the Dead Sea and heals the

Dead Sea. The trees along the river bear much fruit, and their leaves are used for medicine, probably a cure for the bio-weapon jab that is plaguing Israel and the world today. This great miracle of healing the Dead Sea precedes Israel massively expanding her borders in Ezekiel 47 without war. Apparently, the fear of God will take hold around the Middle East, and whatever God says, He gets. I'm hopeful that the remaining Muslims will become devoted followers of Christ Jesus. We have a great opportunity to win the nations as disciples of Jesus at this point of history.

At some point, Jerusalem will be off-limits to Gentiles, for Jesus said the times of the Gentiles would be fulfilled, so it will be wise to mount the most aggressive evangelism early by abiding in Christ and bearing as much fruit as possible amongst the Gentiles for Christ. Moreover, world leaders will be very attentive, as will their citizens, with massive revival and miracles in Israel becoming common knowledge. Several other promises of Egypt being saved and a highway between Syria and Egypt could also happen during this time frame before the rapture of the church and the following great tribulation. Yet the promise of a great falling away (2 Thessalonians) and time of peace and safety (1 Thessalonians) with leisurely living as Christ promised right before the rapture should cause us to warn Christians of these temptation to slide back into worldly living. Jesus made many warnings to those people right before the rapture, and remember Jesus's parable of the fig tree: "This generation shall not pass away until all these things be fulfilled." Therefore, that generation must keep warning and admonishing the next generations and reminding them of all the miracles the Lord did, especially as those forty-nine years (seven weeks) come near to a close, and the Messiah comes as promised in Daniel 9. Remember, the antichrist is on the scene just prior to the rapture with great blasphemies against God (2 Thessalonians). We won't know the day or the hour, but we will have a very close idea when the rapture will happen. Remember the ten virgins parable; they even went out to meet Him. Five were foolish and ran out of the vibrant supply of the Holy Spirit in their lives, and, as a result, they were left behind.

The arrival of Christ in the clouds where every eye can see Him is the greatest event for mankind. It raises the dead in Christ, and those who are alive and remain will be changed in the twinkling of an eye. The rapture has no equal for instantaneous change for evil on planet earth, because the restraining of the Holy Spirit to prevent evil from ruling the world is taken away, but individual salvation will still be abundantly available because whoever calls on the name of the Lord shall be saved. The rapture makes them that are taken incorruptible and waiting out the great tribulation in the New Jerusalem in heaven, even celebrating the marriage supper of the Lamb with Christ.

At the end of the seventieth week of Daniel, those who suffered with Christ will reign with Him and the martyred in the great tribulation. The great tribulation is great rebellion against God and basically God taking creation away from man. There will be 144,000, which is 12,000 from each tribe in Israel, obviously because of the Ezekiel 37 great resurrection of all Israel. These 144,000 will be faithful witnesses and possibly purposeful holdovers who chose by their own free will to miss the rapture; to be faithful witnesses in the great tribulation, and be martyred for their witness. This great tribulation is grievous, but it will produce some fine saints, as are the two witnesses in Jerusalem that are almost indestructible. This seven-year hell on earth separates the good from the bad.

The final return of Jesus is as THE WORD OF GOD and THE KING OF KINGS. It's a fabulous story and very plain reading in Revelation chapters 19 through 22. Then read the first three chapters of Revelation and see the similarities of Jesus dealing with the first-century church and our religious situation today. I've only skimmed the surface of what the Bible says in the latter and last days so as to whet your appetite for your own journey through the Scriptures with the Author. Ezekiel 33–48 is probably the most complete passage of scriptures on the end times in the Old Testament. It seems to be mostly chronological.

Praying to see you in heaven.

A native of Southern California and lover of its natural beauty, Chuck and his wife, Mary, of forty-eight years have four adult married children and twelve grandchildren and one great grandchild. They live in the beautiful Tehachapi Mountains with their family. Chuck works as a successful self-employed designer and builder.

Chuck seems to think Bible and gets right to the biblical solution through his vast knowledge of Scripture and a conversational relationship with Christ. He sees God wanting to be involved with every aspect of life. A story he often tells of trying to design a home without removing a bunch of oaks describes his childlike faith. He stood on the lot and said, "LORD, You're the one who planted all these trees here. How do I put a house here?" The answer was instant: "Where is the view?" He turned to face the view, and then noticed a swath of clear land to his right and left.

Chuck has stood firm for decades against leftists in media, politics, and especially churchianity. His passion for truth is unwavering.